Looking Well *Beyond* Breast Cancer

Carmen B. Marshall

ISBN: 978-1-09834-369-9

About the Author

Leveraging a lifetime of Faith in God, more than a 2 decades of experience positioning solutions related to medical science with such entities as GE Healthcare and Roche Diagnostics, as an Advocate and Activist. Her interest focuses on the unique demands of Women. Wellness is top of mind and how to constantly manage wellness while juggling the demands of life. When she was diagnosed with breast cancer and managed the challenges with grace and poise, looking well beyond breast cancer became the clarion call.

A wife of a 20-year Military Veteran, bringing solutions during an unprecedented time in American History with a viral pandemic consuming hundreds of thousands of lives, much of her advocating took on a temporary virtual face to further reach those in need.

Born to amazing parents, James Lee Brown & Rachel Marie Guerrero Brown, in a small town in Lawnside, New Jersey, her life experiences of overcoming challenges and setbacks came early when her father, who was everything and then some to her, died seemingly suddenly of skin cancer, when she was just 13 years old.

Healing and wholeness has been a mainstay focus throughout her career. As a child, she suffered from asthma. Her frequent visits to the family doctor resulted in immediate relief and peaked her curiosity at a young age. From her early days she always wanted to know what happens to a child's body deprived of air, making it nearly impossible to breath one minute that is relieved instantly.

Hijacked hopes of completing a medical degree to practice medicine after completing a Bachelor's Degree at Rutgers University, staying as close to the profession by career choices gave her a unique perspective of the business of medicine. Advocating in a healthcare industry that moved from giving a doctor the freedom to practice medicine based on years of education and extensive training, to the beginning of governing bodies without such a background, determining medical care, became her mission. As a high performance sales professional, she learned to draw on her career training and layer her life experiences to elevate the importance of making health a priority.

Carmen's desire to understand life at its core lead to her to complete another 4-year degree in Theology, From her childhood and into adulthood, the quest to not just understand the meaning of her life, but also answer questions such as, why bad things happen to good people, is life predestined or are we the masters of our fate, and many others. She served 10 years as a Leader in Interdenomination Organization. The responsibility of organizing and managing teams of more than 120 people in Outreach efforts in the USA and Canada gave her tremendous insights into the uniqueness of each and every individual – men, women, husbands, wives, teenagers, young adults and children. Having a touchstone for truth and a way to measure and weigh life lead to a love for Biblical studies with a view toward teaching people how to apply the principles and understand life's manual. After all, every piece of equipment comes with instructions and her hypothesis remains, if God created man, than surely there must be a guide, a manual to detail how to optimize and function at your best! Carmen credits her looking well beyond breast cancer and thriving beyond a diagnosis of breast cancer to God and being a life learner.

A graduate of Rutgers University with graduate studies at New York University and Wayne State University, 12 years at the bench as a research scientist, followed by academic studies in Biblical research at the former College of Emporia, allows her to bring faith, knowledge and experience in the challenges of today, whether they be physical, mental, or spiritual.

Table of Contents

Dedicated to anyone going through a challenge needing to get to the other side.

And to my husband and all those who have inspired and supported my journey

The Hand Of God Is Orchestrating The Symphony Of Our Lives!

1

Life Happens So Live Through It

In every woman's life there are experiences and incidences that paint a vivid picture and leave a lasting impression in the mind. Your best memory of your father. What you loved most about your mother. The funniest sister and the most challenging brother. Your favorite uncle and the grandmother that seemed distant. Great neighbors and teachers that recognized your gifts and gave encouragement. The first time you became aware that everyone doesn't like you and some will even set out to harm and attack you. The first time you remember being sick and what the road was like to travel back to healthy and being well again. These are just a few of the common experiences we share that we have and will continue to live through until we take our last breath. We just simple embrace with grace, that life happens, and God will give us strength and glory to just live through it!

Have you ever felt like someone is out to get you? You're not alone. In fact, if you are reading this book, there is a very high probability that you are on an invisible list that was contrived quit some time ago. Far before conception, before my grandparents met, before my forefathers came to this country, even before the foundations of the world, that we now know, was formed.

There is a reason for the random hostilities or "happenings" I experienced pretty early on in life. It goes back as far as I can remember. These "happenings" seem to came out of nowhere and bombard my life when I was just living my ordinary, yet extraordinary life. Almost like a colored post-it, these incidence came and my mind start tracking things like, the sudden disappearance of my grandfather from the living room couch. My grandfather, my father's father, lived with my dad, mom and 2 sisters. He was there when I went to sleep and woke each day normally but suddenly disappeared. Another post-it was when the whole town mourned the death of a young beautiful girl named Classie King. She was guiet and kind and liked by everyone. She was a teenager and her and her sisters and only brother were my childhood and family friends. Her 2 older sisters were even our babysitters! This beautiful child died before I reached the 8th grade and I became aware of an entity called death. A memory, a post-it, a horrible fact of life that was not to be ignored.

Here is another post-it...on an intimate Sunday morning, my father and my brothers had left for church and my mother was doing my hair in the kitchen. There was a frantic knock at the door by a stranger telling us to get out the house because it was on fire! Our house was on fire! What? How?

I started to pay attention to these random but related post-its especially when my favorite Uncle died suddenly. I was a candy stripper at the very hospital and again he was there and then gone. Now a huge post-it-worst of all, just months later my mother had to tell us our father had died. All this happened before I was 13 years old! I can still see us all in the front row of the Church. My Mother, now a widow in her thirties with 8 children, many family members, cousins, aunts and uncles, friends, coworkers and well-wishers. I could hardly keep track of what was happening and in fact tried to blink real hard so as to wake myself from a terrible nightmare! It was then, deep inside, quietly I began to get it. Something was indeed out to kill me and destroy my life.

It took many years later to understand I was not wrong. What began as a storybook beginning: loving, hardworking, father that provided for our every need to a proud mother who made sure our home and everything about our life was ordered and lovely, to a routine of eating diner every night together as a family and discussing our day, to going to the same church my grandfather and father with his brothers and one sister went to, to going to help elderly neighbors, to going to get ice cream from a farm where we could feed the animals and watch the horses run to watching 1 TV show only if we didn't fight and argue with each other to a life of organized chaos!

I came to learn sometime later that there is a thief who is coming for all of us. He is coming to steal, kill and absolutely destroy us, if at all possible. It is only when we find the truth and the keys to living that we can withstand these tremendous attacks. I was only 13 when I saw my healthy and strong father disappear for nights at first. My mother protected us from what she may have know and simply said my father was going in to the hospital for test. I knew something was wrong because our family doctor made house calls. Why wasn't Dr. Young able to fix what was wrong with my father? He fixed everything else! I didn't give it much thought until one day, one of my brothers and my sister came home crying so hard I thought their heads would explode. For some reason, even as a young child, I never went to see my father in the hospital. I had seen people in hospital beds and I didn't want to see my father like that. Even when he was home on bed rest with oxygen tanks, I never thought for one minute, he wouldn't get better and return to our normal life! Yet on the front seat of the church that day, there lay some little man in my father's suit. He had died of skin cancer supposedly, having undergone chemotherapy and a number of test at Thomas Jefferson Hospital in Philadelphia, PA. He was not recognizable to me that day, so I looked only once and then looked away telling myself that if I didn't look, it wasn't happening. I went as far as to make up a story in my own mind that he was tired of us kids and my mom and had gone on a vacation but would be back. The preacher that day said God had taken my father home to heaven. I might have been young but from everything my father and mother had taught me to that point, I knew that couldn't be true but I had no tangible proof or teachings to be able to make sense of what was happening. Instead, I contrived a story that said that at some time when we were all behaved and doing all the things he asked us to do, he would return. Somehow this gave me enough peace to focus on going on living but had me looking into the face of men to see if it were him. It wasn't until I learned what God's Word had to say about what had happened that I had an answer of peace. Life lesson: learn the truth from the Word of God, the Bible. This is easier said than done because many believe by being a good person, being nice, serving in a church, going to church, belonging to some religious organization solves or checks this box. It does not. You have to know the Word of God and believe the Word of God. Like the Eunuch in the Bible and many people I meet, that ask the questions, how can I learn the Word of God, you must have some-one teach you, guide you into the all truth.

I was born in the winter of 1958, at Cooper Hospital in Camden, New Jersey. I lived the first 18 years of my life on a street called Mouldy Road in a town called Lawnside, New Jersey.

Lawnside back then was a very special place in the 1950s, 1960s and 1970s. An all-black community, self-governing with a black Mayor, black doctors, black store owners, black dentist, black post-master general and post office, black educators and so much more. Filled with elders, where everyone knew everyone, or at least every family name was known. We knew everyone in our neighborhood and who lived in every house in our little town. There wasn't a house in this less that 2 mile tract of land that you could point to that we all didn't know who lived there.

For a long time, our house and one other, were the only homes on our side of the street. Directly in front of our house was Thomas Avenue. Across the street on each corner were 2 small-framed homes that served as mighty pillars of the community. Mrs. Mary was an elderly woman that sat propped up on a couch where she could look out the window and see what was going down on Mouldy Road and down Thomas Avenue. Ms. Mary was in possession of a mirror she would use to give her a view of the neighborhood, and next to her was her phone where she could call any mother and give a report of any wrongdoing, foul language, or strangers lurking in our neighborhood. With that mirror, she kept a close eye on all the neighborhood kids. During that time the neighborhood consisted of my family-the Brown's, the Stephens, the and Simon's families, and during the summer, the Bunches family. As we got older, the Kings, Williams and Willis families joined the neighborhood. They were there all along but just a block away. Our neighborhood was limited at first to 2 to 3 doors away, then 5 to 6 doors and further, as we got older. Mrs. Mary's daughter, Ms. Alice, was an adult and lived with her and always offered us sweets that we came to know as candy.

On the other corner was the family that kept my sister and me during our preschool days, the Richardson's. They too were an elderly, gentle and kind couple. The Richardson's lived with their daughter, Ms. Tea, and their granddaughter, Nadine. Mrs. Richardson baked the best cinnamon buns that melted in your mouth and had a wonderful taste like nothing I have ever experienced since. Mrs. Richardson would always bake us a birthday cake on our special day. On one occasion, she baked my older sister a pink, heart-shaped cake on her Valentine's Day birthday. Mine was always my favorite … a chocolate cake.

The location of our house was significant. The main cross streets were the White Horse Pike and Warwick Road that ran east and west. Two main highways ran through our town. One is the New Jersey Turnpike and the other is State Highway 295 that runs north and south. Coming off the White Horse Pike, our house lay between a graveyard and a large field of woods. The graveyard has since been closed and our beautiful, wooded lot was transformed a couple times. The playing field was where we gathered for games like softball, football, tag, dodge ball, baseball and hide-and-go-seek. There was a field of trees there initially but at time went on, our field was cleared and we, along with the community of families.

Technology has changed the way children play and engage. Imagination has been stunted by the use of electronic devices for recreation. During my childhood, we were introduced to the art of playing outside. The neighboring woods was my favorite playground and was frequented as my father often took us on magical journeys and hikes. He made it so exciting by teaching me and my family how to make forts and play army. He would show us the value of a fallen trees by using it to make a shelter. We never threw away old blanket as when we made our tepee using 3 trees, we used the blankets as walls and coverings. Once we had our shelter set up, my father would take us on a scouting run to find sassafras plants to make tea. The woods were our favorite place to play as our father taught us how to use our imagination and the resources around us to have fun. The fall was especially fun with the advent of leaves. We would rake them up and dive head first into them making tunnels and hiding places. Funny thing is, we never got poison ivy, poison oak, spider bites or ticks nor did we ever give it a thought! Those woods that once stood tall neighboring our yard were amazing for other reasons too. We would hide our valuable treasures as my Dad had showed us how to mark the trees to find our special location. As with many things, change came and the woods were first partially cleared making way for a perfect, off the street, field where we organized baseball games. Little did we know, the woods were cleared to make way for an apartment complex. Some time between the clearing and the actually building of the complexes, there were enough woods to still run through and organize games. Unfortunately, when somebody became fascinated with matches, the woods were accidentally set on fire. Thank God for Mrs Mary and her mirror because she called the fire department before any real damage could be done. Today, there is a small apartment complex that will forever mark our favorite wooded play area. Life happens so you just learn to adjust and live through it.

Prior to the apartment complex coming, the field was cleared and we used it to play major baseball games. The Wilson family had and equal number of boys and girls and many were much older than my oldest sister. The sons were so talented and often between the families like the Wilson's the Simon's, the Willis' and the one son in the King family, we younger, smaller kids would dream to be selected to be on one of their teams. During those days, the

Borough of Lawnside was a haven for African Americans. A place where young families could grow. A place where generations lived under one roof or at the very least, families resided together – father, mother and children. There was no such thing as a "single mother" in our community. The family unit was intact. All of my classmates had a mother and father. We all knew each others families and could name every one in a household or at least to which family people belonged. We were the "Brownies," different from the other family whose last name was also Brown. My father was known as Brownie so we liked being called a Brownies. At times people would get the 2 families mixed up and we were quick to correct them as being a Brownie was our name and not theirs. In our protected world, little did we know how unique and blessed we were to have such stability. Elders supported our young parents and our parents gave us great stability, care and nurture. A real sense of community and belonging was well established. In Lawnside, New Jersey, we were a closely knit, self-sufficient community. I appreciate attending school from kindergarten through high school with the same group of people and many remain as friends today.

Delaney's was the community store, where Mr. & Mrs. Delaney and their 2 daughters provided a place to buy groceries before supermarkets were a thing. Unheard of today, but you could walk into the store and get whatever you needed without a dime! My mother would send us there with a note and a tab was kept and paid each week. When Mrs. Delaney wasn't looking, Mr. Delaney would give us a piece of candy. Milk and bread trucks delivered right to the front door and fresh fish trucks canvassed the streets in the summer. From time to time, we even rode our bikes in the fog of the mosquito trucks. These were just the way life was for families like mine in the early 60s and 70s. People who looked different from me were seen on occasion, passing by in a car or when we drove our family station wagon outside of Lawnside. When you say Lawnside to anyone living today, many smile and the next words out of their mouths are, "I remember the park and the barbecue."

The Town of Lawnside has a special place in History and was a unique place of many celebrations. I recall the parades every Memorial Day and 4th of July. I cannot remember where the muster point was for the start of the parade, but we always had my relatives come from Philadelphia and have gigantic cook-outs that lasted the weekend. We would set up lawn chairs at our house that sat on a small hill and wait until we could hear the drums as they rounded Evesham Avenue to Thomas Avenue. To this day, I can still close my eyes and feel my heart racing with excitement as if those Boy Scouts, in freshly pressed uniforms would round the corner with the American flag leading the way. It was a time of not be Negros anymore. We were Black Americans. We are Black and we are proud! We displayed our great Black pride with drill teams and organized groups and associations that cared for the community. Groups of children were organized and practiced by older youths of the community who took an interest in shaping our lives.

In our part of the world, we had our own Beyonce long before anyone knew she existed. The Sissy Pilots, Bonita Richardsons and Monzata Wilsons, of our small town, were nothing short of amazingly beautiful, smart and talented! They were mentors long before it was a common term in our vocabulary helping us to put our best foot forward. There I was, shiny knees lifted with white boots decorated with white tassels swaying to and fro. A different set of matching tee shirts and shorts strutting to a cadence with synchronized clapping and stepping together gave distinction to the our various groups. Fire trucks, police cars and the Ambulance would sound their sirens and the proud Masons and Eastern Stars walked with dignity in finely pressed uniforms. The women wore white gloves. The Boy Scouts displayed badges sewn just right, displaying their accomplishments. Mrs. Picou's group of Girl Scouts and Brownies had their sashes pressed to perfection, hair perfectly platted and marching tall, carrying banners and flags. As the parade would get to the top of Thomas Avenue and Mouldy Road, all performances, sirens and noises would stop. A somber group in uniforms carrying flags would go to Mount Peace, the graveyard next to our house and decorate the graves of fallen soldiers with fresh new flags that would wave long into the breeze as the seasons changed.

I don't know about you, but from my eyes, Lawnside was special, unique and nearly sacred to those of us who were fortunate enough to grow up there. Walk with me back to a time when we caught lighting bugs in jars at dust...not fireflies. Shoes were optional in the summer as you ran down the street or played games like hopscotch, tag, 1-2-3 red light and more. You always said hello to everyone and waved as people passed by in a car. We said things like Y'all as if it were a proper noun and if you used the word 'aint' you were corrected immediately. Your play clothes were the hand me downs that were too small to wear anywhere official. Playing and having fun was always outside -never inside and in front of a TV or radio. When we got thirsty, we drank from the garden hose, icy cold refreshing water! We ate what was cooked by our mother's and we were never asked about what we wanted to eat. There wasn't even the notion or option of not eating and going to bed as punishment for not eating your dinner. You sat at the table until you had finished your food. At best, you prayed to have a dog that you could toss the peas and carrots to without getting caught. We ate fruit from from our own or the neighbors trees – apples, pears, cherries, tomatoes, water melons and grapes. All sports were played on grass, dirt and concrete only if we were on school grounds. We were not afraid of much except stray, loose dogs. Like most, in the summer, the streets lights coming on signaled time to go home or at least play in your own yard or at least close enough to be seen and or heard if your mother called for you. If you DISRESPECT your elders, there were consequences and repercussions as everyone knew everyone and the report got back to your parents without social media, only a landline. Not unusual to get POPPED with whatever was close by for misbehaving. Best of all 4th of July meant a huge parade that you were in either by way of a drill team, the scouts, decorated bike rider or ran alongside any new additions to the parade that had cute boys.

So much has changed in my hometown of Lawnside since that magical time. So many wonderful people have fallen asleep permanently and now await the Lord's return. If you are from Lawnside, you are among those who had the good fortune to develop from a rich household and heritage in what was once one of the best places for young Black families to thrive and grow. The last noted change was when the house I grew up in at 139 Mouldy Road was torn down. If you drive down the street today, you would never know there was so much life, love, support, encouragement and fun that happened at this address.

The house that resided at 139 Mouldy Road was originally built on the White Horse Pike. It may be gone, even my father, himself is gone, my childhood now long gone, but the many wonderful memories, the joy of a good life and the pain of loss, the happy times and the impact of the many lives and living that is in the rear-view mirror continues the process that life happens so you just live through it!

James L. Brown

Rachel M (Guerrero) Brown

II Corinthians 2:9 – Holy Bible, King James Version

...as it is written, Eye hath not seen, nor ear heard, neither have entered into the heart of man, the things which GOD hath prepared for them that love him.

II Corinthians 2:9 – Holy Bible, Amplified Version

(without exact punctuation)

...as the scripture says, what eye has not seen and ear has not heard and has not entered into the heart of man, all that GOD has prepared, made and keeps ready, for those who love Him, who hold Him in affectionate reverence, promptly obeying Him and gratefully recognizing the benefits He has bestowed.

2

The Diamond Mindset

A diamond has multiple facets and what makes it shine is the light that hits it at a certain angle. To get the maximum sparkle, you have to have the light hit the right angle. The origin of a diamond comes from the Greek word Adamas, which means indestructible or invincible. You've heard people say pressure makes diamonds, well, that is indeed a fact. Light is needed to give a diamond its shine. Light hits the diamond and the bounce-back effect is what gives the shine you see when you look at the stone. There are light and dark areas of a diamond. The dark areas are needed to achieve that beautiful shine and attractive sparkle that gives a diamond its value. Just like a candle seems brightest in a dark room, the make-up of a diamond uses this concept to shine. A gemologist I am not, but I want to describe the characteristic fires or facets of my life that gives me my shine.

Growing up in a household with my father, James and my mother, Rachel, 2 older sisters, Rochelle and Althea, who we called by here middle name - Lynn, and 5 younger brothers, James, Carlton, Kenneth, Tyrone and Reginald, was nothing short of an amazingly wonderful experience and launching pad for life, These facets of my life were filled with various celebrations, community activity, and clubs and associations to help define and refine as many social graces as life could pack into me. This is a facet

My father worked hard, leaving the house in the early morning after my mother prepared him breakfast. Back then, we used instant coffee and I am not talking about something that comes out of a Keurig or the drive thru at Starbucks. No, not even an app can get this kind of coffee. I'm referring to a cup of instant, Sanka coffee. My father was known as Deacon Brown to those associated with the church and he served faithfully at the Baptist Church he, his father and 2 brothers helped to build. On Wednesday night there was Bible Study and Thursday night was Choir practice. I can still close my eyes and hear him singing "In The Garden" or his voice cracking as he prayed reverently. I didn't understand until much later in life that he was praying and petitioning God for us, his children, his wife, his church family, the sick and the shut in, the lost, the aging, the hopeless, the fatherless and a host of other things. He was a caring man and he knew how to cast them on to God so he could get on with living. This facet of my life serves as an an anchor to this day.

I don't know how he managed a family, caring for his aging father, mentoring and advising his 2 brothers, working both a full-time and a few part-time jobs, cultivating good friendships, being a leader in his Church and community as well as supporting his extended family. An important part of developing a diamond mind-set is to learn how to set priorities and make time for what's import-ant to you.

My father demonstrated by his life that children have to learn to share their parents and parents have to recognize when and how to share their children! Neither is easy because we each want all the love, affection and attention. He was a hands-on dad. My father was proud of his 5 sons and took great pleasure spending time with them. Something me and my sister, Lynn, sometimes wished we were boys so we could have that kind of attention. My father spent time coaching his sons and the community of young men in baseball and football. He served as a Cub Scout and Boy Scout leader. He kept an immaculate yard and vegetable garden and always made special time for us, his kids.

I am reminded that that there was not 8 children all at once, something my mother use to remind us of and it makes sense. We came in stages and when it was just my 2 sisters and 2 brothers, life seemed pretty darn perfect. How could it not be as from my eyes, I was the special one. I was the 'baby girl' that last daughter before the sons and the dividing line between the girls and the boys. My first friend was my sister Lynn and my second friend was my brother Jamie. My father spent time teaching and training us, while having fun and spending quality time. We weren't rich financially, but the richness of life stays with me to this day. My father took the time to really see us for who we were as individuals. He knew our strengths and weakness. He seemed to see our future and guide us differently so as to help us on our journey of life. It was my mother who cultivated our intellect and fostered our learning skills, but my father put the polish on. One of my favorite memories of my father was a saying that stays with me until this day.. He would often say.."if I told you once, I've told you a thousand times". I didn't know what it meant as a child and it took many years later that I fully comprehended its meaning. A critical facet in my shine was comprehending when instructions are being given, to pay very close attention and not allow my mind to drift. I learned to listen intently so as to retain the words spoken and carry it out repeating what was said over and over again.

Teen Years

Haddon Heights High School
Senior Picture

In a diamond, the darkness is there. Like most parents, my parents gave me great values and tried to cultivate a virtuous character and content in me, however, as I grew up and went on to college, I picked up a few 'dark' habits. I am not proud of this but the even bad decisions taught me how to use life lessons and keep shining. Let me tell you more about this particular facet.

I remember the time and a particular situation when I was with a certain group of people where I suddenly started lying about who I was. The lie was so easy to tell and rolled off my tongue that it was out in the universe before I could stop it! Its like it had a life all its own. I thought I was an honest person and I thought I told the truth but in fact, certain situations just called for a fabrication, an embellishment and a highly exaggeration of the facts.

One particular non-truth I often share to help others, I told for many, many years. When I omit information or strategically place my words, it can indeed result in a non-truth. When asked did you go to college, of course I would answer yes, however, if asked did you graduate from college, well, here is the story. In my early twenties, I told people I graduated from college when I hadn't. While the truth is that I have earned my Bachelor's from Rutgers University in New Brunswick, NJ, there was a time when I used my college experience and 116 credits to answer affirmatively that I had graduated from college. To graduate from Rutgers, you need 120 credits. As I was advancing my career and gaining experience applying my scientific understanding in labs focused in medical science, I wanted to pivot to a sales career. An opportunity presented itself and I was offered my first position as a Technical Account Manager. I was thrilled. My manager was going to be an African American man, highly intelligent, managing multi-millions in assets and the most lucrative aspect of the new corporation I was looking to join. He was offering me an opportunity to join his team and assume positioning our solution to a major pharmaceutical company. This would be the first time I would have a company car, an expense account and the ability to work from a home office. I was over the moon happy!

My life at this point was pretty amazing. I was in a great relationship with my now husband, enjoying success in my career. This was major considering I had taken a hiatus from the lab and research to work and dedicated my life to God and sharing the Word of God full-time. This meant I spent years living on a need basis with no extras. Now I was resuming my career as if I had not taken a little more than a decade off to do what amounts to missionary work here in the US & Canada. I had closed on my first home. It was a bank-owned property that was purchased, remodeled and enjoyed for 5 years and sold for a 33% profit so when I landed my first major opportunity career wise, I was single, in an amazing relationship, driving a beautiful automobile with hair that grew out of my scalp, that was down my back! Life was nice, comfortable and I was on the come up!!!

The job offer documents arrived and I immediately completed them, drove to get my drug test and waited for the offer that was now countersigned to be executed. When I received the call to come into the home office in Mt Laurel, New Jersey, I was already planning how I would leave my car there and drive the company car home, come back later with my hubby and pick up my vehicle. My soon to be new bosses Admin Assistant, asked me to have a seat and the Manager would be with me shortly. I loved the warm reception and the excitement she shared about having me join the company. What came next came as a surprise, dare I say, shock, when I heard the words,…"we were not able to verify your college graduate status so would you have a copy of your degree?" He went on to say that without the ability to verify my degree, the job offer could not be extended! My heart sank to my feet. At that instant, I realized and was reminded that there was a facet of my life that was unfinished. I had accepted the non-truth myself. I believed this non-truth for so long that it became my reality. With my self-made reality fully embraced, modeled and displayed, I was accepted and give opportunities in science that helped to shape the person I am today as a career consultant to research scientist, however, now I was being held accountable! Ever hear of that saying, what's done in the dark will come light? Well the light was on!!!

What happened next is nothing short of God's grace and mercy. Losing my father so early in my life meant that when I went off to college, I had to have a plan to take care of myself because my mother had 5 more children after me to care for. Losing her husband and being left to pick up the pieces took its toll on all of us, including my mother but that's part of the facets of my life. A diamond doesn't shine without any light and so was this facet of my life. The life lesson here was no matter what we tell ourselves, God knows the truth and just waits for us to come around.

The promises made by God are available and do not depend on what you do or don't do but is directly dependent on God's willingness and ability to do for us! God has promised us that he would never allow us to be in any situation where He will not make a way for us to not only get through the challenge but do so in a fashion where we come out more than just okay. The facet that illuminates the most is that angle where you come to the realization that no matter what situation arises, trusting God allows us to shine. That's the diamond mindset!

Here is what happened next after the second shoe dropped, figuratively. I was a student at the University where my student number was 426XXX. During college, I was never treated any other way than as a number, but God made it available for me to connect with an Advocate at Rutgers. This was a woman who worked with me to get the few credits I needed to complete my Bachelor's degree! Yes, I had gone to college, I had successfully completed 116 credits, but 120 was needed to graduate. Needless to say, I graduated and have my degree matted and framed in my office today! The diamond mindset reminds me that life has many facets. Holding yourself accountable in the presence of God helps determine how bright that aspect of your life shines. I could have run and hid as I felt so foolish that day, sitting in my soon to be new Managers Office, but instead, I owned up to my mistake and was able to shine on!

The diamond mindset, in part, is being able to turn the situation at hand in such a way that you see your true self and the situation at hand in the right light. Whatever the situation or challenge facing you today, the lessons you keep with you may be needed in the future. The diamond mindset is a lesson in how to take charge of your life! You may have heard from various sources that no one is coming to save you. I intuitively knew this and trusted my relationship with God. I believed, as you should too, that God will never leave or forsake you. Find out how to get your faith up and trust in Him. People will always let you down and disappoint you but its not people you must rely on. Yes, that Manager gave me an opportunity as I was offered the position with a contingency. The offer was contingent on me getting my degree in short order, which I was able to do. To re-enroll find an Advocate and get through the process at the University where more than 50K students are attending was nothing short of God.

In order to get the shine, I needed, much like a diamond, I had to keep turning the situation to God, doing my part, until I received the brilliance I needed. Never give up, even when it looks like things may not work out in your favor. That's the diamond mindset!

In my 20's.

Dreams

LANGSTON HUGHES

Hold fast to dreams
For if dreams die
Life is a broken-winged bird
That cannot fly.

Hold fast to dreams
For when dreams go
Life is a barren field
Frozen with snow.

…a poem my mother taught me to memorize
as she often taught me by reading to me
from authors such as Langston Hughes, Richard Wright
and James Baldwin

…a poem I later recited at a 7th grade assembly
as a love of the written word was further developed
by the greatest educator that ever lived, Mrs. Helen Morales

3

What Is Your Body Telling You

What an amazing feeling as you see the finish line to a process. That's what I think of when I think of graduating from secondary school, or what some call High School. Few things compare to the excitement of closing a chapter of your life to embark on an unknown journey filled with many turns, figurative traffic circles, fast highways and several slow country roads. Even some parking lots. So it was when I was graduating from High School. Haddon Heights High School, to be exact. This is the time I began to start to come into myself and recognize I had my own likes and dislikes separate from my family and friends. Experiences began to shape what I liked. What I was good at. Who might be a real friend? This and other concepts began to shape who I am almost as with invisible hands.

During High School, I took a course in Home Economics. This was on the top floor of the school with 4 small kitchenettes on one side of the room and 4 large sewing tables on the other end of the room. One Instructor for both classes. A lovely, mature woman who gave instructions in cooking and sewing. The class was mixed with freshman and upperclassmen so the conversations around the mock-kitchens and sewing table, always landed on boys. I learned how to make my own prom dress – cape and all and also learned how to make lasagna. I also learned about sex in the back seat of a car, playing hooky with boys when parents weren't home, and older men available to have sex although they were married. My ability to look like I wasn't paying attention but actually all the while ear-hustling conversations, gave me the most interesting bits of information. I learned s0me of my classmates were sexually active and who had no intentions of going to college, dispute their parent insistence. Instead, they told stories of boys, men who loved them and promised them the world. Some of the more mature girls spoke of starting a family. I was just a Freshman and these conversations of a few were contrary to what my mother expected of me. Between the talk in Home Economics and instructions in Sex Education my understanding of sex, intercourse and orgasms was only on the pages of a book Somewhere in my Junior/Senior year I too had a few stories to tell.

In college, one of my favorite classes in college was an elective in Women's Studies where our textbook was **Our Bodies, Ourselves**. During the class, I experienced my first woman's wellness exam. This was adding to my body of knowledge that started with my mother, added to by my older girl cousins and classmates on the top floor of the High School. The care of my body and knowing every detail of it had many blank spaces. I believe I had my first visit to a Gynecologist once I was in college. I registered for a Women's Studies class taught by 2 very incredible women. The syllabus covered every phase of a women's development, sexual identity (only straight or gay were the options – sexually fluid and LGBTQ had not made its way to center stage), relationships, the importance of sexual health, reproductive choices, childbearing and post reproductive years. The main textbook was Our Bodies, Our Selves, by The Boston Women's Health Book Collective. The material was so helpful that I still own a copy, a newer edition, of course, as a reference. Every woman and girl should own a copy.

There is no question that everyone needs a good education, knowledgeable teachers and champions, able to speak intelligently and dispense sound advice without judgment. This class taught me all about a women's body. An actual full examination was performed using a live model to explain and demonstrate how to perform a breast exam, the difference between the labia minor and labia major, and the clitoris. We discussed Roe v. Wade, the landmark decision of the Supreme Court protecting the rights of a pregnant woman. The instructors gave students the option to 'opt out' of these progressive 'labs' and conveyed that students could leave at any time if they felt uncomfortable. There was a Board-certified Physician conducting and explaining the exams and the reasons for each step as the Instructors search our curious faces for ease. The model walked into the room where she was greeted by a nurse. The nurse modeled the bedside manner of what we, as women, should expect to expect as she described the procedures. Then the Doctor entered and again displayed what one should encounter. We were all still teenagers, so we had the discussion of how to ask for a female doctor if we were uncomfortable with a male Doctor. Regardless of the doctor's gender, we were instructed that a second person should always be in the room when being examined. The exam covered the basics of checking vitals. The Nurse was asked by the Doctor to remain in the room. The model/patient was asked to undress completely and put on a hospital gown. The class was showed what a breast exam should look and feel like and how to perform a breast self-exam. This is a class every young girl should have to know what is appropriate and what is not appropriate. I still remember my near shock as the doctor told us about what a healthy vagina should look like and how a healthy vagina smells. Then the model/patient prepped for a vaginal exam. It was done in groups of 3-4 women using a speculum and I learned at 18 what a pap smear was and why it is part of a routine examination. As I look back, I remember how at that time, I felt embarrassed that I was uncomfortable, ashamed I was so ignorant and uncomfortable looking at a women's intimate anatomy. That class changed my life because I was so ignorant of my own body. The class was a huge success in that I learned my body and how to pay attention to it as early as age 18.

My mother taught me how to be a girl, a female and a woman and that these 3 aspects were all different. As a young girl, she made sure my sisters and I knew all the social graces as each attended what was called charm-school. She impressed upon me the importance of education and reading. Sometimes her words of describing a girl, a female and a woman took on different verbal colors and at times seemed harsh and crude. Being a full-grown woman today, I understand what she meant and it's not something you can learn from a text book but has more to do with the learning in the classroom of life. There are aspects of being a woman that have to be embraced, owned and comprehended and that only happens with time and experience-your experience or learning from others.

At 83-years old, my mother had only been hospitalized to bring another sibling into this world. She rarely caught colds and may have had the flu once in my lifetime. I am unaware of her ever taking any medications, even to take something if and when she even had a headache. That's healthy and to stay that way she always said things like 'stop watching and paying attention to all those pill commercials because they telegraph all kinds of sickness. If you listen long enough, you'll start thinking you have what they are talking about and should start taking the pills just to be on the safe side.

Later in life, after my mother was nearly 80 years old, she fell down concrete stairs outside my sister's house and broke the largest bone in her body, her femur bone. At the time, I was living 3 ½ hours away. My sister, brother-in-law and Niece all present at the time of the incident and now were calling me in hysterics. They passed the phone around and each person was even more unclear as to why my mother what screaming in the background. Once I got the Hospital name and which Emergency Room she was in, I contacted the nursing station. I was not surprised when I was informed my mother was threatening to hobble out of the hospital. The nurse informed me of the extent of the damage, and I knew her demanding that her leg just be wrapped up and she be released was not going to happen, so I immediately started the drive to New Jersey.

Driving north on Interstate, I-95 gave me time to settle myself and rehearse how she had always taken great care of herself and was in great shape. There would be nothing to fear and that we would be there to support her through the process. I knew I would have to have a good explanation for why she needed the surgery to counter her usual argument that doctors were practicing medicine. I knew it was going to take God's help to get her through this challenging situation. I prayed and asked God for wisdom on how to handle this very situation, To say my mother was apprehensive about surgery of any kind can best be understood if you knew how her belief system was, hospitals were places people go to die. I had believing and trust in God that all would be well. After all, my mother's body was telling her, her femur bone needed repair and that could only happen with surgery.

It's important to keep good physical records of visits to the doctor's office, results of all blood work, reports of each x-ray, Ultrasound, MRI, CT Scans and all matters relating to your health and wellbeing. My mother's surgery went well, and the next step was rehabilitation for 6 to 8 weeks. When I visited my mom, I noticed her nightstand was filled with pills. When I asked her where the pills came from, she said she would pretend to take the medication given her by the staff, but as soon as the nurse would look away, she would spit them out or drop them and then hide them in the drawer. My mother shared she didn't want to get hooked on the medication, so she didn't take the pills, and no one checked to confirm that she did! When I asked her about the pain, she said she would rather live with the pain than to risk becoming dependent on pills to get through her day. Then she went on to say, she saw the staff roll a dead body out one night and knew she wanted to live. That night she said she was determined; she was leaving after only 2 weeks. At points she refused a cane, walker or any assistance and slowly put weight on that leg. This sounded crazy at the time but today, she plays with her great grandson, walks and runs without even the slightest effect that at one point her femur bone was cracked! When it comes to knowing your body, like my mother, you have to have the courage to recognize what is right for you and not get talked out of your believe system during a crisis!

In my 30's.

My mother taught me many things and among them was, how to always be a fighter. Fight to be heard. Fight to get your point across, Fight for what you believe in and most importantly, fight for your life! After her own prescribed stay of a few weeks, she checked herself out of the rehab and was home in her one-bedroom apartment that has 3 steps to the front door and then another three or four steps to the single level unit. What stayed with me was something we both laugh about and that is, watching dead people roll by or reading obituaries daily only cause you to think more about your own mortality. Our conversations today focus on a theme we both adopted from the experience...'Why sit or live around those dying when you want to live!

Know yourself and know your body. That means when you feel or intuitively know something is wrong, don't ignore it. Don t be afraid to seek help. Around age 26, I was told by my Gynecologist that I had uterine fibroid s. These are benign tumors that grow inside the uterine wall. My normal menstrual cycle was every 30 days and lasted only 3 days with no discomfort or cramping. Every now and then, I would experience a little discomfort in my lower abdomen. A few days of having to wear my 'fat clothes' due to the usual water weight gain. The growth of fibroid tumors are slow but by my late 40's, during a workout, I laid on my stomach and , it felt like I was laying on a golf ball. As time progressed, it felt like that golf ball was growing and becoming a soft ball. Still, the worst symptom was I had to start buying larger sizes to fit my waist. I was a newlywed with no desire to have children. I was healthy, worked out regularly, ate a balanced diet and took very good care of myself. During my annual women's wellness checkup, a Ultrasound study revealed the tumors were pressing up into my diaphragm and pushing down on my urethra.

My life was perfect and all was well but there was an inner voice that kept at me to consider taking action about these seemingly harmless tumors that were growing. My body was telling me it was time to act soon, even though I was asymptomatic. I sought recommendations from trusted friends and colleagues. I interviewed a select few of physicians as if I was a Board Member of a Hospital asking about their credentials, successful surgeries and outcomes. It was important to partner with a trusted Physician and not just any physician. This was when I began to develop a passion for advocating for wellness for myself and soon every woman I came in contact with. I found the perfect doctor for me after 'interviewing several' to find a match in values, in procedures, in bed-side manner, and personality. Wendy Martinez, MD., was my choice because when she entered the room, she was the embodiment of a healthy woman and more importantly, she gave me additional things to consider not assuming I would use her service. I also really liked her woman-friendly approach to wellness. She was the first physician to ever mention bringing in another specialist, a Urologist, because of the close proximity of the fibroid s to my bladder. I knew I would have a trusted advisor that was skilled with an excellent bedside manner. In the event, there were issues beyond her expertise that needed to be addressed, she had the expertise in the room with her. The surgery was a success and I felt amazing about the decision I made to act. It was the knowing my body and trusting what some call intuition, but I know it is the God in Christ in me.

Life was happening and I was taking notes along the way, keeping careful track of these important events and all the details prior, during and after. The surgery was called a uterine myomectomy and was my first surgery. I read everything I could to prepared for the surgery. Additionally, I started going for longer walks, eating more fiber and vegetables. Days before, I purchased a juicer and began juicing. Surgery time, I was ready. I was married and my husband took the journey with me. He was there when they rolled me into the OR and was the first voice I heard as I came out of anesthesia. My first thought was, thank you God! My next thought was help me Lord because it hurt to sneeze, cough and even laugh. Three days in the hospital and I was home. My husband had made a beautiful bedroom around our fireplace on the first floor so I wouldn't have to climb the stairs. He waited on me hand and knees. My body and life were telling me that God is love and that I was loved. Love is essential to make it through a crisis or any challenge.

In my 40's.
Carmen Brown &
Michael Marshall.

As a woman, I would rarely think of myself, if at all. I have had a job and then a career since my first job at the Elizabeth E. Crawford's Child Care Center on Warwick, Rd in Lawnside, NJ.

Caring for and about others has been an essential component of my work, my passion and my skills that can be documented as far back as the 8th grade. In the 9th grade I was a hospital volunteer known back then as a Candy-stripper, at Our Lady of Lourdes Hospital in Camden, NJ – an unpaid job that required me to use public transportation, the Bus, to get to and from work. This early experience prepared me for a hospital visit as I knew what a Unit Clerk was, the difference between the various nursing credentials and their authority to give care. I didn't understand it then but by the time I needed surgery, I fully comprehended that healthcare is a business and before I was admitted, there were several questions and facts that were essential for me to know. All hospitals are not equal and do not offer the same level of care. That being said, while its critical to know what your body is telling you, its paramount to know all you can about the doctors, the staff, the facility and their process prior to needing care.

My recovery from a modified hysterectomy took fewer than 3 weeks. I know it was all because of God's favor, God's mercy and grace on my life. It was how God was at work within me, guiding me to do and understand what I have described. I listened to what my body was telling me. This would all help in the coming years because I was diagnosed with breast cancer a few years later and had to undergo several surgeries, chemotherapy, radiation and adjuvant treatment. I knew my body. I trusted what God had worked in me and I was unafraid to act. When the time came, it was easy to look back and feel like David in the Bible. I had slew the Lion and the Bear and now Goliath was at the door.

Michael & Carmen Marshall

Proverbs 22:6

Train up a child
in the way he should go;
and when he is old,
he will not depart from it.
— K J V

Carmen (age 3), James L (father), James (age 1) & (Althea) Lynn (age 5)

4

DNA to Your Whole Self

In the womb, you are in darkness, how dark, I am not sure as my conscious brain was not developed to record such environmental conditions. However, until a woman gives birth, all the unborn can experience is partial experiences of the mother. Once born the experiences become our own and leave deposits in our being that can forever change us. Often those engagement and interaction leaving evidence of the exchange. One very important moment came with Mrs. McGlester, my second-grade teacher, whom I absolutely loved and adored. This astute educator encouraged my love for reading and the written word that is part of my very DNA. My mother was an avid reader and there were books throughout our house: a gigantic white faux leather Bible, a series of Encyclopedias, multiple dictionaries, hard cover novels and many paperback books. Back then even the giant catalogs that came from flagship stores like J.C. Penny's, Bamburgers, John Wanamaker's, Litt Brothers, Strawbridge's & Clothier and Sears & Roebuck, was used by my mother to teach and to instruct. We used these sales catalogs not to shop but to learn how to spell words and diagram sentences. We also used these various sources to read out loud. As children we occupied our time practicing math by adding up totals from the sale prices and being asked what could we afford with X number of dollars. Many of the things I love and enjoy can be sequenced back to my parents and these innocent learning experiences that was so much fun.

Each Fall, I looked forward to going back to school to do what came nature to me and that was to learn. It's a quality that was nurtured in me at an early age. The best part of going back to school was getting assigned your books. The books were given out at the beginning of the school year and students were responsible to steward those books until the end of the year. I sat patiently waiting for permission from my teacher to even open to the first page. The binding and the pages seemed magical. The books were used for multiple classes and had a place for students to sign their name and take ownership for that year. I could not wait to see who had read the book the years before me, and I grew even more excited if the ledger was full because that meant a brand-new book!

I cared for my books as if they were golden because for me, they held secrets to a life I had not experienced. It was not normal for students to take the books home, but I remember sneaking mine home from time-to-time. I would go to my room and make sure it was clean and everything put away. I would use my hands to iron every wrinkle out on my bed and then sit on the floor beside the bed and retrieve whatever book I had smuggled away. I would turn the pages and look at the pictures. They were pictures of blond hair, blue-eyed children, dressed adorably with pets and toys. They were always happy looking. That was the "Dick and Jane" series. It was many years later that I wandered why the children did not look like me.

I loved the words and short stories. I would spend time practicing reading out loud so when I went to school, my pronunciation and enunciation would be perfect. I would print out the words and practice for spelling tests. Once I found a box of new books in the coat closet of Mrs. McGlester's class. I opened the box and took a book home under my coat. I did not know at the time that I was stealing by taking something without asking. When I told my mother what I had done, she disciplined me and marched me back to the school and made me tell Mrs. McGlester what I had done and had me admit my crime and apologize in front of the whole class. I thought I would die of embarrassment, but what happened next was nothing short of amazing. Mrs. McGlester told me I could keep the book. Wow! My very own Book to have and keep at home! This was better than Christmas and my mother allowed it.

I learned an important life lessons that day which stays with me to this day. Number one, if I want something, just ask for it. Resist the temptation to take matters into my own hands. Number two, it is okay to make mistakes and it doesn't matter who knows it. Just own up to it and be prepared to accept the consequences and responsibilities. And number three, and probably the most important, God's mercy is so amazing that you need not be afraid to own up to your mistakes. These were my formative building blocks upon which my whole self is constructed.

In Lawnside, New Jersey, a small community of African Americans, where my teachers and all the support staff were all African Americans. The Elementary School went from K to the 8th grade. Classes were divided into the A & B class. Around the 4th grade, I looked forward to my teacher announcing, "Time for Bible Study". This was the signal for the class to line up, in alphabetical order, on one side of the classroom, and begin to walk down the hall, down a flight of steps, out the side door of the school building and across the street to the Lawnside Borough Hall. "No talking," the teacher would instruct. "Shhh" each child would pass down the line until there was complete silence. The only sound was the click-clack of the 15-18 children's feet moving in order down the hall. When we arrived at the Borough Hall, we were assembled again and given direction to move in silence to a seat ... no pushing or passing. The teacher would then count us one at a time until the row was full. No one dared utter a word. Once seated, our teacher would release us into the care of one Mrs. Rhoda Scott. Mrs Scott was a gentile woman. She would enter and welcome us to Bible Study. Later I came to realize that we were in the Court Room of the Borough Hall. The row of seats went all the way up to the Judge's bench.

Bible Study was a large part of my early education curriculum. It took place less than a few yards away from the school in a separate building. It was their lessons about God and His Son, Jesus Christ, were taught. We had green, Gideon Bibles that contained the New Testament. Over the years, we learned the books of the New Testament and how to spell them. We had drills where we would find verses of scripture by chapter and verse. "Who can find John 3:16? The first one to find it, please stand up and read it." We nearly tore up the pages of our new Bibles searching for the scripture. Everyone participated and, as far back as I can remember, everyone enjoyed the drills. The student who could find the scripture first was rewarded for success. The gifts seemed better than silver or gold - a pencil with a beautiful ribbon, a handmade bookmark, or something else to encourage participation and success. No food or drinks were ever involved, and not everyone received a reward. Children who could not perform to standard were given more attention and if that didn't work, the child would be left behind and allowed to repeat the grade. We had to do the work, practice and learn. Even in Bible School, there was a standard and it was upheld. We had to learn the Books of the Bible. Recite them in order and spell them correctly. We had drills and to win prizes. Needless to say, I won many special prizes, and this added to my being as I enjoyed winning. I wasn't selfish with my winning. I would share prizes and often help my nearby classmates.

At the time of this book being written, violence in schools – school shootings and such other horrors are an all too real events in our society. In our little sequestered town where everyone knew everyone, we all looked very similar and everyone worshiped the same God and confessed Jesus Christ as Lord, and this kept our community free of the disasters that befall our youth today. If one checks the police blotter from those times, 1963 to 1972 in the Borough of Lawnside, the worst thing that ever happened was a car full of white boys riding through Lawnside yelling, "niggers." I only recall this happening once. Another time, a pack of stray dogs came from nowhere and chased all the children in the neighborhood. Checking with the Volunteer Fire Department would verify an incident that occurred when Mrs. Porter's house caught on fire. If social media was available back then, this wouldn't even interest 2 followers! That was it as far as violence or odd occurrences were concerned. There were no robberies, no shootings, no children being kidnapped or hit by a car, no known domestic violence or events that would make the evening news.

Interestingly, I do not even recall a single Muslim family in the entire community. My first introduction of a non-Christian came in college. I was curious and even tried to experience the faith, reading the Koran and listening to college friends as we would share their beliefs. My DNA is that of a woman that trust God and has confessed Jesus Christ as my Lord and Savior. Like many in my community, we worshiped under the same or different denominations, but the same God. We may have differed in our traditions and religious practices, Baptist, Methodist, Lutheran or Roman Catholicism … those were the choices, and nothing else.

My first impression of the Black Muslims came when I began college at Rutgers University. My thoughts were, where do I sign up! The men wore suits on campus or at least a tie and shirt. They were extremely articulate and could speak all night without ever repeating themselves. The lifestyle of the Muslims I came in contact with compared to the other students on campus was that they denounced the use of drugs and alcohol. I remember just being totally infatuated by these handsome, smart and well-dressed men. When one guy named Hakeem approached me, I was all ears. He was an Engineering student and we often crossed paths on then Busch campus. The courtship was a process that started with encouraging me to join the Nation of Islam. He would meet me outside my building and walk across campus with me to the cafeteria. After dark, he always walked me to my dorm, making sure I arrive safely. I lived in a co-ed dorm but Hakeem never came to my room. He shared how it would be inappropriate. He was from Newark, New Jersey and a very wise young man, however, the courting process came to a screeching halt when I asked him about Jesus Christ. He gave me many references of the identity of Christ as a prophet but stated rather emphatically that Mohamed was that prophet. I am sad in one respect to report that our relationship ended abruptly because this was a deal breaker for me. Jesus Christ was already coded in my DNA.

It begs the question or at the very least should put for consideration – what we have really done with all of this freedom our forefathers and many men and women fought so hard for to grant and protect! Why have we made so many changes to the educational system and who has benefited from it? Who suffers? What kind of society are we creating for our children and grandchildren? What is the legacy they will inherit?

I cherished the learning and appreciated the power of words from as far back as the second grade. In later years, Hakeem used the power of words to seduce me and I enjoyed every minute of our time together. Our paths parted but I thank God for the Hakeem's of the world. Black men that stand out and stand up for what they believe and desire to protect and educate their community. He was my 'Barack Obama' in his manner of speaking during my college days. He worked hard at getting his education and encouraged many of us to do likewise. The goal was to go back and build up our communities. The love of words that form sentences and generate images in the mind still is a powerful force. The seeds were planted early by my parents, fostered through elementary, secondary and college years and continues to be the thread that holds my life together.

5

Imagineer The Life You Want

Imagineering is a concept and a tool whereby I use my mind to conceive of futures that I would bring into reality. It's a combination of the word imagination and engineering. In my youth, when someone described me as having on rose colored glasses inferring that my way of seeing life was not as it actually was, little did they know, they were observing my early stages of Imagineering. Described as living in a fantasy world was also another phrase attributed to my being. What I now know for sure is that I used my imagination to engineer scenarios and situations that I wanted to be a reality.

Sometime during graduate studies, I understood that the brain is not able to tell the difference between a vividly imagined event and an actual lived event. I wanted to test this hypothesis using an exhortation from the Bible, in essence to ask and believe that we have the things we ask of God. I spent considerable time imagining and engineering the life I wanted to manifest as early as my twenties and its something I practice to this day. Imagineering can be used as a powerful tool. Have knowledge of yourself and direct yourself to a better life.

New York University Medical Center on First Avenue in Manhattan posted a position for a Lab Manager in the Neuroscience

& Physiology Department. I use to imagine as I watched the actress, Marlo Thomas, starring in a show called That Girl that one day, I too would be That Girl. I would walk beneath the Empire State Building and look up to see the top. It would be me walking down 5th Avenue window shopping and moving in a rush to get to work among the businessmen and women making things happen on Madison Avenue. It wasn't long before I had a regular window seat on the Amtrak train from New Jersey to New York. I would exit with a flood of people when the doors opened at Grand Central Station. Each day never seemed the same as I looked out on the Manhattan skyline as we drew closer to the city. As early as age, I saw myself as a brown skinned version of the character Marlo Thomas played. The theme song began to describe not Marlo Thomas but me and before long it was me working odd jobs looking for my big break. The big break came when I was offered the job to work at NYU as a Lab Manager, my first realization that Imagineering really works!

A key component in Imagineering is the ability to be very clear about your goal. I reached a point in my life where my goal was to make a drastic change in my life and living. I wanted to move out of the metro NY area, away from the hustle and bustle that I once craved and ran to years previously that now I felt the need to escape. I moved to Detroit, Michigan. A place where I knew no one and no one knew me. Prior to doing so, I was a classic work-a-colic so I had nearly 6 weeks of vacation pay and a modest savings. I ended a dead-end 5-year relationship, sold everything in my apartment and subleased my beautiful living space to a friend. Packed 2 suit cases and boxed my books and personal items requesting they be shipped once I was settled. Where would I live and better yet, where would I work?

Time alone to sort through my life and be out of the earshot of sirens from the urban jungle, I stopped along the way to capture my thoughts. Under a sunny tree at a rest stop, I began to write down the type of house I wanted to live in, not an apartment and visualize the neighborhood of custom homes I saw in magazines. I had a catalog of furniture and fine things in the imagination of my mind. I envisioned a college atmosphere where diversity and the quest for learning was the norm, Friendly people with strong cultural roots that would accept a Jersey Brown Girl filled my heart. Within 2 weeks I had a job at Wayne State Medical Center and rented a Tudor Home in Palmer Woods between 7 and 8 Mile Roads. I had the pictures of my life and held them in a special compartment until they were a reality.

An important aspect of being successful at Imagineering is to develop what I call a persona that only you and God know about. Children sometimes make imaginary friends, and some may take issue with this practice. A positive and constructive aspect of this practice is, it allows for private conversations and discussions with yourself to help crystallize ideas, play out different 'what if' scenarios and construct a workable action plan. God hears of every word and thought so it is a planning session, a private counselor, a confidant that will never reveal your secrets until you are ready. It is indeed you!

Freud's psychoanalytical theory describes the human psyche or personality as having 3 parts. The parts are called the id, the ego and the superego. One article conveyed the id as an instinct, the ego as reality and the superego as a moral compass. The Aesop fables cartoon watched as a child often portrayed an angel-like advisor encouraging you to do the right thing on one shoulder and an evil, pitch-forked demon encouraging a poor decision. The cartoon was used to show the mind at a crossroad. Somewhere in between my life and living I used these concepts together to make what I called 'my trusted advisor." This was a persona that I consulted when I had to make difficult and complex decisions. I had learned early in life, that there are just certain things about my life I didn't need to ever utter to another living soul. Having the ability to imagineer using my trusted advisor is what I used to move more than 600 miles from the northeast to the mid-west.

Imagineering is a powerful tool God has given me to use for His glory. It's a skill I had been developing and perfecting. The reality of the matter is that is that it served me as proof that God would always make a way for me so when I was diagnosed with breast cancer, I knew exactly what to do. Everyone has a story and here is mine: **Mrs. Marshall, is your husband with you?** the doctor asked. She was a Breast Specialist referral from my OB-Gyn Specialist. After reviewing my mammogram and performing a physical exam-ination, the recommendation was to perform a fine needle biopsy of a suspicious area. I can still see her face as she announced . . . **You have breast cancer**.

My trusted advisor and I began to rehearse a few facts that seemed relevant at the time. My paternal and maternal grandparents combined had 16 children and 47 grandchildren, of which, I was one of those grandchildren and not one of the 64 in our tribe had breast cancer. I knew Imagineering was going to be a necessary aspect of my recovery. The words of Psalms 118:17 helped me steer my thinking and calm my spirit reminding me that it was possible to have God's promise in the midst of my challenge. I set my mind that I would not die but use my story to share how to move from a diagnosis to deliverance and restoration.

Important components required to fully envelop Imagineering is recall and rehearsal. This is when I use my mind to recall important events similar to the situation I found myself in. One example, and there are many, I once prayed for a friend's mother who needed open heart surgery. Circumstances were such that I was able to share my faith with her mother and a few instances where the hand of God rescued me. I asked her if she had accepted Jesus Christ as her Lord & Savior. She confessed and received that God was a God of healing and that He would heal her. A few days later during her pre-op testing, the doctors told her the blockage had been cleared and surgery was no longer needed. We knew it was God and thanked and praised God every time we saw each other.

Imagineering goes back to the Bible and the record of David who slew the lion and the bear before he took on Goliath. I am almost positive David reminded himself of the successes he had with God against an enemy. Perhaps he replayed those images in his mind before he went up against Goliath. Sitting alone in the doctor's office, I imagined this and thought of records in the Bible where God had healed people of their malady. I though on the engineer of my being, Almighty God. I rehearsed how God is a healer, a way maker, a life changer, a situational adjuster, a deliverer. I began to recall how God is faithful and had brought deliverance and healing to me, from things as simple as a headache to more complex issues such as lack and loneliness. All I had to do was ask, in the name of Jesus Christ and believed His Word.

Imagineering the life I wanted had worked well prior to this office visit. I was well trained and in top shape. I wore a dress size in the single digits! I had regular, annual check-ups and always received normal, healthy reports. Clinically, my risk factors were nonexistent! What was she saying? The doctor was back, and her voice interrupted my fellowship… Can we make arrangements for someone to drive you home? With news of this nature, you should not get behind the wheel. Do you need tissues? The doctor and her nurse navigator stood looking at me as they may have done countless times and watched patients completely unravel. They had not seen such a reaction or lack of reaction when they announced to a patient that they had cancer. I received the report of their findings with the confidence of the Shunammite woman in II Kings 4, facing a difficult situation who responded to Gehazi 'all is well'…I told myself over and over…it will be well! I was escorted to an office and asked to wait. It seemed like time stood still waiting to ask questions and speak about the next steps. That little devil from Aesop fables jumped in suggesting I was going to die young like my father. But God had me well prepared as I had the rock of all ages, the rock Christ Jesus and now with the rock, Christ Jesus, I would have the power to quench all the fiery darts of the wicked, evil one! Satan is the author of death. Satan, the Adversary steals health, strength, and prosperity. When you read these chapters in the Bible, Ezekiel 28/Isaiah 14, its clear to understand the rogue behavior of Satan. His lack of character, his fall as once being an angel of light. He is jealous, envious, rebellious, mischievous, slick, conniving, and always wants to be in charge ---just like cancer cells. He is the great counterfeit! The word of God says we are fearfully and wonderfully made! God designed our bodies and instituted cell division as a normal process for the body to grow and repair itself. Healthy cells stop dividing when no longer needed. Cancer cells keep going and going. Cancer is Satan's attempt at copying God's masterpiece. After all, Satan still wants to be like the most High God. He takes 1 rogue cell, turns to 2, 4, 16, 256, 65, 536…keep doing the math and you can easily see how tumors are formed.

Thinking about what the Word of God said about this situation ran through my mind as the doctor continued her report and detailed next steps. On the outside, I was living "…eye hath not seen nor ear heard, neither has entered into the heart of a man the things that God has prepared for them that love Him!" (I Cor 2:9) I had just purchased my first house, was a joint-heir of the grace of God with my husband, had been given a brand-new company car and was working my dream job that took me into the labs of the top Pharmaceutical Labs at Merck, Bristol Myers Squibb and Johnson & Johnson, just to name a few. I had traveled to France, Germany, Switzerland and so many places in the US and Canada! All because of God's grace and mercy on my life. I had built years of trusting and believing God. I was humbled and appreciative of the truth that God does not deal with us after our sins or reward us according to our iniquities. So like David, who slew the lion and the bear, I was ready for Goliath!

I began to collect all the surgical reports related to the diagnosis of breast cancer, the radiology images and every blood test run by the lab for review by a customer's husband, the Radiology Director at the Medical Center at Princeton. I remember looking around the waiting area and taking note of every woman. Some seated by themselves as I was, others with their husbands and a few with what might have been a friend. What arrested my attention were the frail looking women with scarfs on their heads. A couple of women were completely bald, and I could tell it was not by choice. After mentally cataloging the people, I then start to take note of the furnishings. I had already known that healthcare is a business. I have since come to know that cancer is a money maker, so it's no wonder treatment centers have stunning high-end art, well-appointed furniture, and magazines. The designs are there to bring comfort or to offer beautiful distractions. What was always missing was a Bible or scriptural references. I began to imagineer magazine covers with a subheading that read, "He lead captivity captive and gave gifts unto men". I replaced the expensive works like that of Richard Royal's Waterford pieces with mounted and framed "…through death Jesus Christ destroyed the power of the devil" Perhaps at check-in they could have "The thief comes to steal, kill and destroy but Jesus Christ came so we could have life and have it more abundantly" Maybe if more scriptures where on the walls, then patients could understand that indeed a crime was being committed against them. The thief was out to steal health and if he could, kill us! Maybe, just maybe, instead of a diagram of how to escape in case of fire, they could post the scripture of Psalm 139:8 that states, if I make my bed in hell, thou are there!

When I have been in the battle for my life, I knew I needed something greater than myself. I chose the God I knew. God's Word states there is nothing new under the sun. Two things I knew for sure as I was getting a second opinion: cancer is not new and God's ability to deliver is not new. I had to be in Boston for meetings that following month so I made arrangement to get a 3rd opinion at the Dana Farber Cancer Institute in Boston, MA. My diagnosis was confirmed and the action that seem right for me after careful deliberation was to seek aggressive treatment.

First order of business was to get out my Bible Concordance and look up every record in the word of God about healing. I knew and confessed that God had not changed and still today, has not changed. I looked up and read as many scriptures as I could: The Woman with the issue of blood, those healed of leprosy, the blind men who received their sight, Peter's mother, The Centurion's daughter, the man at the temple gate that asked for alms, the man with the withered hand that stretched it forth, even an accident when the dude fell out the window while listening to Paul preach. Maybe my next Book will be those pages that I read and rehearsed the days following.

Next, I organized a binder, scriptures first, neatly typed out, next blood test, surgical reports, radiology reports and nutritional information. I carried it to every appointment and took careful notes.

It was time to tell my husband. That's right...I didn't tell my husband or anyone. Not my mother, sisters, brothers or friends. Something I delayed until I had my heart and head conditioned with the Word of God and was confident of the direction I wanted to take. I didn't tell my loving supportive husband up until now because both my husband's parents had died of cancer at an early age. I prayed and practiced how I would deliver the message to assure him all would be well.

My husband had spent 20 years in the military, but my immensely strong husband cried and hugged my neck so tight I think we were both hardly breathing. I shared with him my binder of scriptures. We read the word together and acted to shut out the world. Only TV and radio with teachings from God's Word and healing, encouraging music. (My CD)

It was now time to act:

- 3 Surgeries – I maintained a sense of humor the whole time, learning and telling jokes to my care givers and thanking God for a hedge of protection before falling off to sleep. I always looked at the clock and had a conversation with God that ended with me telling him I looked forward to continuing our conversation when I wake up, before slipping off to sleep

- 8 rounds of chemotherapy – each time they stuck a needle in my veins, I rehearsed, the life of the flesh was in the blood. I imagined the blood of Jesus Christ cleansing me.

- 27 cycles of radiation –

On a stainless-steel table, alone, in a dimly lit room, the feeling I felt that morning was similar to a feeling I had had before. It was similar to the time I managed a lab at New York University on First Ave, down from the United Nations. I lived in East Orange NJ. That morning, I had only enough money to get to work but no money to get home. I prayed for God to see me through and off to work I went. Around 2 pm that November day, I noticed it had started to snow. The city was different. I notice my colleague who usually worked late, locking up her lab. It was snowing harder and was starting to accumulate quickly so I too started to leave. I was so busy with work, I had forgotten I had no money and no ride home. New York City and New Jersey is separated by the Hudson River. You must drive over a bridge, go through a tunnel, catch a bus or train or swim. I was acting as if I already had what I had asked for, so I headed up First Ave, toward Penn Station. I had a lot to overcome because it wasn't snowing when I left that morning, so I only had shoes on. No hat, no gloves, and no scarf! It was so cold the leather soles of my shoes cracked, and the ice cold water made it hard for me to feel my feet. After a few blocks, I started to cry. In desperation I started asking complete strangers for spare changes. They walked by without missing a stride as if I were invisible. One lady even yelled, 'get away from me' as if I were a bum. With all the hustle and bustle of people making their way to the trains its a wonder I could hear anything. I heard Ting Ting Tink and looked down. There was a coin. At first it looked as if it were sealed in the blacktop but when I fished it out, I walked to the train, inserted my coin and was able to get home. During one of those 27 days of radiation, I remembered various, incidence, some far worst, yet God had sent that token from heaven so I was confident he would bring me through as He always had.

God made dry bones come to life in Ezekiel, Cancer is no match for Him! I'm writing my story to encourage other women to look well beyond the diagnosis of breast cancer. After more than 16 years in the doctor's office I am sharing my journey to bring awareness that God is a healer and a deliverer! He did it for me and He is not a respecter of persons.

6

Purposeful Living

When I thought that I might die, a thought that only came to my mind when I was diagnosed with breast cancer, I decided to start living again and not leave my fate in the hands of others. In my 5th year of survival ship, my motto I shared with everyone I came in contact with was 'get busy living or get busy dying, either way, get busy! To jump start the process, I went back to an exercise from elementary school when the teacher asked the class to take out a piece of paper from your desk, not a table but a stand-alone piece of real estate you owned from 8 am to 3 pm from the 1st to the 5th grade. Use a freshly sharpened No. 2 pencil, not an iPad or computer and write an essay answering the questions, "Who am I." I cannot recall exactly what I wrote then, but this has become an important component of survivor ship. I often do this exercise, maybe once a year or so to guide my journey throughout different stages of my life. By doing this simple exercise, it was a way that lead to purposeful living

In every woman's lifetime there are common experiences and incidences that leave vivid pictures on the canvas of the mind. Purposeful living requires an element of recall from this vast library of favorite memories and times that, when I looked back, emoted a smile and a lift to my heart. One childhood memory that stays with me are the summer's early morning laundry days. Summertime in the early 1960s was quite different from the summer times of today. No WIFI enabled devices accessed by ThinQ technology, no washers run via an iPhone or Android devices or not even Siri could help. No, I'm talking about a washing machine with a ringer. Maytag made a basic tub with 2 large rolling pins on top. Connect a hose for water and a second for draining. Wash, rinse and roll garments through the wringer to catch the now damp article. While the spin cycle got most of the water out of the clothes, feeding the clothes between the 2 roller pins and watching the water run back into the washer and the almost dry garment hit the basket involved manual intervention. This process required focused and multitasking could result in a few crushed fingers or worst yet a possible electric shock!

Summer laundry days on the back porch of 139 meant taking an approach to laundry more like a game. I must credit my mother for her imaginative way to give us a supporting role and purpose in getting the laundry done. Incorporate my sister Lynn and brother Jamie into her work routine, if we did not lose all the clothes pins throwing them at each other, was to hang each piece of clothing on a clothes line. We often darted in and out between the sheets. Our job was to be the commander of the clothes pins and eventually evolved to actually hanging the clothes. To this day, there is nothing that smells as fresh as cloths that have basked in the days sunshine. Fresh sunshine, air dried laundry cant be bottled. This whole memory serves as a reminder of experiences that happen early in life that rarely register as significant yet become part of my favorite memories when I think of purposeful living.

My mother directed the affairs of our household with purpose. What I loved the most was that she allowed for games to be played between chores and often came up with the games. Quite ingenious looking back as this kept us occupied, engaged and helped to get the work done. If she was doing something that required her attention, we played a game she called dumb school. We had 12-14 stairs to the second story with a landing that went in 2 different directions. My Mom started the game as the teacher with us sitting on the landing. She would hold a marble in one hand behind her back, out of our sight and ask a question. We took turns, one at a time trying to select the right hand that concealed the marble in her clinched fist. We were to answer the questions correctly to graduate to the next grade, which was the next ascending step. If you missed the question, you were left back. Easy questions and appropriate questions for our ages such as name all the aunts and uncles, to answering a math question, to spelling states, name the presidents, and on and on. This taught us to pay attention, enjoy learning and to compete to be the best regardless of our age. My mother called it dumb school to set the stage for real school. She would tell us if we didn't do well, being left back was a possibility. We knew by playing this game what it felt like to be left behind, which in turn encouraged us to excel. The object of the game was to ascend to the top of the stairs by answering each question posed correctly to then become the teacher. The teacher could ask their own set of questions, vetted by my mother, of course, as she was always within earshot of our games. Purposeful living has elements of inclusion and fairness.

As our family expanded and I became mature enough to take on more responsibilities, laundry moved to the local public laundromat. We did not own a dryer and once school started, there wasn't time to do laundry as in the summer. This new workflow meant gathering all the family's dirty cloths and using my Uncles

Army duffle bags, outfitted with coins and cash to wash, dry, fold and resort the clothes before bringing them home. By now the family consisted of my parents, my 2 sisters and 5 brothers, and my purpose evolved as a contributor. What became my signature was being mindful of others and time management. I used time between cycles to plan out my future house, complete with a washer and dryer.

I came to be born in a historical African American or Black Town of Lawnside, once called Snow Hill, then Free Haven before Quakers named the town as part of the Underground Railroad. My father and his father, came from Lindenwold, NJ. The house in Lindenwold, known as Grandpop's house, caught fire and burned down. My father was young and I was told everything was lost - all pictures, memorabilia, and traces of their existence. From Lindenwold to Lawnside my grandfather, adult father and adolescent younger brother moved. My mother was born in Philadelphia and is 1 of 13 children. She once shared with me how important it was for her to have her own husband, her own house and her own children. My father met and married my mother, took care of his aging father and younger brother before my sister Rochelle was born. Knowing my parent's beginning and journey gave a sense of direction and helped guide my path and set goals to chart during my life's journey.

South Jersey in the late 1940s and early 1950s was made of small towns where farmers brought their goods to sell in Philadelphia. Eventually a road was paved known as the White Horse Pike. Today there is a Home Depot and Lawnside Shopping Plaza where once houses were. After the houses were moved, there was a large drive-in movie theater and a large white Horse was placed on the lot. But before this happened, to make way for the growing commerce, the houses had to be moved. My father purchased land in Lawnside and then one of the houses that was for sales. During those days, houses were not demolished. A new foundation was poured and the structure was moved to what became 139 Mouldy Road. The house I grew up in and lived in until I went off to college was once built on Route 30 or the White Horse Pike. If you go by this parcel of land, the house is gone and the property ravished with no sign of life, not even a squirrel. Bad things happen to good people every day and I had a front row seat to much of this before I got to college. I did my best to live through it and draw on the best parts to arrive at a purposeful life.

In the spring of 1970, that house that my parents made a wonderful home for me, my brothers and sisters, caught fire. At the time, the shock of it all temporarily erased the facts that my father lost his mother as a young boy, then lived through his childhood home burning down. One Sunday morning, my father and brothers had gone to church and my mother was ironing and curling my hair in the kitchen when a passerby notice smoke coming out of the attic window. My youngest brother Reggie, sister Lynn, and I waited at the neighbors and could hear my mother directing the fire department on how to extinguish the fire. No one was injured and thanks to my mother, our house sustained minimal damage by water. The great relationships and care we enjoyed in our little universe allowed friends of the family to house us temporarily. The fire started in the attic so as soon as the roof was repaired, my father re-constructed the living space so we could continue our purpose as The Browns.

Growing up in a secure, 2-parent household, gave me great security and comfort. I took so much for granted starting with the notion that my life would always be pleasant. Even if and when a crisis arose, my father and mother were talented and resourceful enough to protect us. That all started to shift just before a Thanksgiving holiday when my Uncle Skip died. He was just at our house weeks before and then gone. Before the next Memorial Day holiday, my father died! My favorite Uncle and my first love, my father, gone and I was just starting High School. Thankfully, so much love, knowledge, virtue and beauty had been poured into my life that I knew my purpose in life, or so I thought.

Purposefully living comes with many significant emotional events that bring learning and validate your existence. One notable event happened in the winter of 1984. This was a day during my post college times and I was finishing scientific experiments in the lab. I was so busy that I hadn't noticed that it had started to snow. I had arrived at work with no way to get home. I was penniless and that was not a figure of speech. In New York City with all it glitzes and glamour, I had to make my way home to S. Munn Avenue in East Orange, New Jersey. My coat was stained and needed to go to the dry cleaners, but I hadn't the money to get it done. I was hungry and cold by the time I started to make my way home. That morning as I headed into the lab, the weather was much different, so I had no gloves, no hat, no scarf or boots. Out my window, the snowflakes seemed endless. I was high above the hustle and bustle on the 17th floor so I hadn't realized that more than 2 feet of snow had fallen in a short period of time. Slush on the sidewalk, and layers of dirt and grunge mixed in by the snowplows and shoved wherever there was space. "Excuse me, ma'am. I need money to get home. Can you spare some change?" A hard, cold look up and down with body language suggesting I should not take another step closer. Not so much as a brake in her stride ... I was dismissed by a glare.

It took a lot of strength for me to even get up the nerve to talk to strangers in Manhattan for money. Here I was, a former Rutgers University student, working for a Principle Investigator at a prestigious institution at New York University Medical School as a research associate in the Department of Neuroscience, begging for money. This extremely emotional event was the result of a series of bad decisions. Purposeful living comes after as the result of traversing a number of pivotal crossroads.

I arrived at this particular crossroad in 1980 when I was supposed to be graduating from Rutgers. After my freshman year in college, I was put on academic probation because I was not able to manage my course load that included biology, chemistry, calculus and chemistry with other courses, a 30 hour a week job and a boyfriend. The boyfriend was eliminated by default as he already had a commitment with another girl and a baby on the way back in his hometown. This impacted my mental state as he had as been a trusted friend and protector. Every girl can benefit from an admirer who is strong, smart, good looking and on goal oriented when attending college. There are so many people looking to take advantage of the naive, wide-eyed with wonder, ready to take on the world type of girl, entering into a college setting. Despite his obligations we remained good friends. The proof of our unique friendship came when a "hotshot" basketball star invited me to his room, which was across the hall from my friend. He proceeded to try to rape me balling up his fist to strike me when my friend heard the commotion and kicked the guy's door down and beat the living crap out of him. I was hysterical and deeply traumatized. My friend brought me to his room, and we sat and talked for hours. He checked on me each day, walking me to my classes, sitting with me in the dining hall and more, until I felt safe. Why had nothing been done to the basketball player? How come no one else seem to be bothered by what had happened as word went around campus among my peers. Could it be this was normal for some people? I started to question my purpose and plans.

College is a place of higher learning and indeed I learned life lessons that guides my life to this day. I share my experiences in hopes to help prepare others for what awaits when leaving home for the first time. I am a first-generation college graduate. I was supposed to have mastery and disciple to manage my life only to find that the effects of losing my father so early stage in my life left me vulnerable. My mother was navigating her life as a 38-year-old mother left to raise the remaining 5 boys at home. It was now, at a time when I needed her most, her priorities were shifted, and I was left questioning my purpose and my plans. These circumstances seemed to be insurmountable obstacles that challenged everything I had come to know and trust to this point.

Rutgers University had a student population of over 50K, and my core classes had hundreds of students. This layered my life with yet another level of complexity making it a real challenge to focus. Having been raised and educated in a small town where I was accustomed to being the top student or at least one of the top students to this environment required more support that I had at the time. There were so many foreign students, mixed with adults, in a culturally rich and developing cite of New Brunswick, NJ. Very few people among the thousands knew my name as opposed to my home community where I was well known and respected. As an honor student in High School, I was involved clubs and associations from American Field Service to the Varsity Club. Even with a part-time job after school and extra-curricular participation, I maintained my status as an Honor Student, graduating in the top 5 percent of my class of 281 students! However, now in a completely new terrain I was struggling to keep up. No one prepared me for the transition from a class size that maxed out at 15 to now more than a couple hundred student. The educators were not teachers but teaching assistants, better known as TAs. The TAs were working on graduate degrees, some of which did not speak English well enough to teach the alphabet, let alone chemistry, biology and calculus. At the opposite end of the spectrum, there was the excitement of wanting to grow socially as I was meeting so many new people from every ethnicity and culture. I was particularly intrigued by the "upward bound" students from the inner cities. They were not only fun, but intellectuals, highly motivated and had drive and purpose that impressed me. I attached myself to a group that had what I didn't - a well-developed social network to support them during their college years.

I started college a few weeks after graduating from High School as part of a special program entitled EOF for Educational Opportunity Fund. It was a program that focused on low-income, first generation college students interested in health professions. Medical School was top of mind. I worked really hard to finish high school well and start college on a high note. During summer orientation as an EOF student, I made friends with 2 girls who had graduated together from the same High School. They were not friends in HS but it made sense to me that they should be and so I found a purpose in uniting them so the 3 of us could be friends. Looking back, I can see why they were not friends. One was wise beyond her years having grown up in an environment where her mother was a bar maid and the other growing up in a strict 2-parent household, the three of us shared the fact that we were the first generation to attend college.

College parties were held in the student Union with enormous dance floors and a time when the nerds, the athletes and the successfully social all came together to have a good time. A highlight of the parties was partner dancing a style called the Hustle. My one friend was a very well sought after dance partner because she "hustle" well enough to win the "Dancing with the Stars" Mirror Ball Trophy. Whenever we got together in our dorms, she often interrupted our study time encouraging us to learn to the dance. She spent hours attempting to show us how to follow her lead. Often, her room was filled with the cutest guys who willing came to help her practice. She was well known on the campus among the athletes, and various groups of guys. The style of dance, which some called hand dancing or Chicago style dancing, was the type of dance where my friend could dance with multiple partners. It was as if she was a modern-day Josephine Baker, Debbie Allen, or Misty Copeland, though not formally trained. Her beauty and poise would always cause the crown to form a circle around her and her partner or partners and be entertain by the magnificence of this style of dance, very unique on a college campus dance floor. This captivated my attention, as it brought me back to my ballet lessons in my formative years that I really loved. Besides wanting to be a Doctor, I secretly wanted to dance for the New York Ballet Company. Purposeful living allows for more than just one goal or desire. In college many of my friends and other African American students preferred to dance and party together, passing on getting wasted as a college pass time.

I have always loved dancing and this new style of dancing was no exception. I sacrificed studying to spend more time learning to dance rather than getting tutored to to keep pace with my core courses. Looking back, I can't recall my dancing friend ever buying books or going to class. It's no wander she wasn't able to return after the break from the Spring Semester of our Freshman year. Still, I allowed myself to follow this passion for dance pushing the words that had hurt my heart so early on, 'you will never be a ballerina because you are a Negro girl.'

When our friend didn't return for the next semester, we knew we had to be roommates to keep each other on track. It was a little too late for me as I had gone on academic probation and began to question my purpose. How would I get to Medical School now and often had many sleepless nights trying to catch up on my course work, Juxtaposition was all the attention we received from upper classmen? While 2 of the 3 of us could be classified as silly and immature, we were all attractive. Football players, basketball players, players of all kinds hung around our dorm and always made room for us when we came into the cafeteria. One upperclassman looked out for us like a big brother. Once, my roommate and I decided to learn how to drink. We were inexperienced and prior to college we never had an alcoholic beverage or experimented with the social drug of the campus, aka marijuana. We asked these guys what we should try and they suggested Mad Dog 20/20. They said be sure to mix it with another beverage known as Brass Monkey. Off we went to an upper class-man's room to submit our order. Once we had the goods, we went to our room and began mixing the 2 drinks as instructed. Between the both of us we could not drink get through 1/3 of 1 glass because we could not stop laughing. The guys who told us what to do thought by getting us to drink they could take advantage of us and get us in bed. Were they ever surprised to find out that the concoction simply mad us loud and bold enough to laugh them right out of our dorm, embarrassing them? Our Big Brother heard the commotion and came to see what was going on. When the guys confessed, he gave them clear instruction. After this incident our popularity rose even more. Having a protector and someone looking out for you when you don't even know how to look out for yourself is a key ingredient to living purposefully.

College exposed corruption and chaos that I had not know coming from my sequestered world. From the liquor ordeal we moved to marijuana. I do not remember who, where, when or how, but I do remember smoking my first joint. I was always very serious and uptight and noticed a more relaxed, conversational persona in social settings. I became adept at asking high end questions and being comfortable with meeting new people, At times it was as if I were Oprah before there was an Oprah Winfred. My studies continued to suffer and it took everything inside of me to report to the Dean's office for an academic discussion. I was told that I had 2 options; either withdraw for the semester and return during the summer or continue my studies and risk being dropped academically from the University which would permanently prevent me from ever returning! I was devastated to say the least.

I left college and moved back home. I had taken enough science courses to get a job as a Bacteriologist. This was my first official job offer. The Lab was short-handed, and my basic microbiology knowledge was enough since the protocols were already written. The salary was so great I briefly considered not going back to my college life. I returned to college socializing, working full-time and going to school full-time. I was behind in the amount of credits I needed to graduate, so I leveraged my lab experience to refocus on medicine and healthcare.

By the time 1980 rolled around my peers had already graduated. My job in the Vivarium at the Medical School put me in company with Med Students and re-ignited my passion for medicine and healthcare. Piscataway, New Jersey. I started working with animals that were part of research projects. I started as a Animal Caretaker where I was responsible to to feed them, clean their cages and eventually sacrifice them when the studies were concluded. Animals are used for drug studies and their organs are removed and the tissue prepared for a Pathologist to report his finds to the Study Chief. It wasn't long before I was promoted to Histology and learned a skill set that served me well for nearly 12 years. It wasn't long before I was working at one of the largest Teaching Hospitals for a well-know team of Pathologist, where I was invited to sit with the Medical Residents, Interns and Medical Students as they were trained in the progression of disease. My curiosity always drove me to want to learn more about the human body. When asked if I wanted to accept a role in a pilot program as a Pathologist Assistant, I jumped at the opportunity. This feed directly into my purpose of obtaining a medical education. I was able to participate and eventually perform autopsies. Sitting with teams of medical professionals discussing human disease processes sparked questions of life I had not entertained up unto this point. Listening to the clinical histories and circumstances of life as it progresses to death and what that looks like at a cellular level inspired me to request my father's pathology reports and try to understand how a Black man dies of skin cancer.

The conflicts that raged inside my head as I had a front row seat to lifeless bodies. The questioning going back to my early bout with asthma where I could hardly breathe and then be restored again. What was the medication that worked on me as a child? Why were we not able to save everyone. As I questioned seasoned Pathologist, Nurses, laboratory Staff, friends, colleagues, I was searching for the real meaning of life, my life! I knew it was time to move on from this world because I started having re-occurring nightmares about my father. The last straw was when we were starting an autopsy on this very small, frail, elderly Black woman. It was my personal practice to always cover their face. I did this so I could focus on the biology and shut off my emotions, which always went to the love ones left behind. As I read the chart, this was no ordinary Black woman. This was a woman in my college community that had opened her home during the holidays to support and feed students like myself that decided not to go home for the holidays. I knew her and the disease had ravished her body. I excused myself and went to the ladies' room to wash the tears from my eyes and to ask God for answers. All I could do as I waited on God, was get another job and get out of that Hospital!

I decided at this point to call my sister. We had no contact for for several years. She had taken a job in Arizona after college and was now living in Nebraska. We were able to reconnect when I remembered a visit home to during our respective college breaks and her and my mother got into a heated debate. They had opposing viewpoints on Max Ehrmann's piece Desiderata. This is an amazing piece and my mother use to have us memorize it. The point of contention was the phrase, 'be at peace with God, whatever you conceive Him to be.' My sister was adamant about God and had scriptural references of who God is. She was impressive as my mother is THE GREAT DEBATER! My sister Lynn knew God and gave us all a lesson about the true one, our Heavenly Father. What she share stayed with me. What she had shared with us all bubbled up in my heart and was what I remembered as the thief she told us about was reeking havoc on my life.

That day, I called home to get her number. My sister had always been the great protector and my biggest cheerleader. She gave me encouragement my entire life, When I had to leave college it was her who said get a job in your field of science. I love her for many reasons, but especially because of her confidence in God and her relationship with Him at a time I needed Him most.

We had not spoken in many years and it was just comforting to hear her voice. She was in Omaha at the time. I thought in my ignorance, "What is a Black woman doing in Nebraska?" When we connected, she told me flat out that Jesus Christ had paid the price for my life by dying on the cross and therefore, it was not for sale.

We spoke often and each time she shared the Word of God. Not your typical Bible totter or quoter but practical, common sense truths from the Bible. I never knew the Bible could be so resourceful. Having spent years in histology, a science that requires a microscope to visualize cells, I knew the more you magnify something, the more details you can visualize. I began to study the Bible and use it as my foundation to live my life. It's important to note that God answered all my questions up to that point. As I continue to live a purposeful life, more questions arise. I put them on my spiritual hat rack and wait on God.

7

My Rose-Colored Glasses are Actually Pink

My mother always said that I see life through rose colored glasses. Well, like most mothers, she was not completely wrong as she just got the shade wrong. No matter what was happening in my life, in the world around me or even on the entire planet, I have had the ability to see the good. Not only can I see the good, I actually look for the best part. Now I am no saint, I can be petty, unforgiving and critical at times and I try not to make excuses when I display these traits. I recognize my weaknesses and use them to make changes and choices.

This book is about how I was able to look well beyond breast cancer and see a full life. I pray to God that you never get breast cancer or that the people you love do not have to deal with such a diagnosis. Know that whether its breast cancer or some other life altering situation, such as COVID, it's important to set sights well beyond the immediate. It may help to think of any diagnosis or challenge in life as a snapshot. I choose not to have the diagnosis or the thing that's happening to define my life.

After surviving the high wall, undergoing several surgeries, chemotherapy, radiation and adjuvant treatment, I wanted my life to make a difference. I wanted my talent, my education, my experiences to all be synthesized and focused. Once I was able to get clear and concerned, I started looking for career opportunities that matched my DNA. Disease prevention is the goal, but I wanted to know when disease happens, how do I know that it is there. How do I or doctors know exactly what it is, How will they determine the severity. What will be used to treat the disease and how will we know that the treatment was effective.

I started a unique position with a company as a Specialist. I was able to meet and form relationships with some of the best doctors in the world. What I am about to share is breast health knowledge that is readily available. Some of it comes from training sessions I have participated in while other aspects have come from reputable journals and website. Better still, I have lived through it personally as a breast cancer survivor and have gathered data over the years from many experts.

I like to quote my favorite doc, Dr. Rachel Brem, who holds many distinguishing titles. Her story is her story to tell. Dr. Brem is committed to saving lives starting with her own, as a breast cancer survivor. As a survivor myself, I understand this deeper today and it only adds to my understanding of how information can save a life.

Interesting fact I learned while getting my Degree in Theology is that the people of God are destroyed because they lack an accurate knowledge of God and His willingness and ability to deliver us from any situation. A lack of knowledge can lead to wrong choices and may end life as it is known. I am fully aware that as a reader of my experiences, some may not have the faith to believe for healing and deliverance from breast cancer. To them, I say, simply pray to God that He helps you where you are not believing fully. I often have to ask God to help me too.

Pink is one of my favorite colors and we tend to see pink more during the month of October. In October there is an elevate awareness of breast cancer and more effort around caring for those effected by the disease. Charities such as the Brem Foundation local to the Washington, D.C. area, the American Cancer Society & Susan G. Komen Foundation more nationally, and the Breast Cancer Research Foundation globally have all been established to promote breast screening using mammography and other tools to help detect breast cancer. Continued education and research to understand the cause and support to help those affected by the disease is a multi-billion dollar enterprise. As a survivor, breast health something I advocate for beyond the month of October as women's wellness is a 365-day passion!

I'm an expert of my body and I can state unapologetic ally that it is crucial to get an annual mammogram starting at age 40 and even earlier if there is a history of breast cancer. Have a detailed discussion with your Doctor and give them as much history as you know so together the best care can be planned for you. Its important to not allow COVID or crowd your schedule. Try not to skip years and when you go for an appointment, if you don't go to the same location, make sure you have at least two years of priors mammograms on a CD to take with you to the appointment. This is extremely important as the reading radiologist should have them so that they can look for any changes from years prior. You should also know there are two types of mammograms. The first is called a screening mammogram and if the screening mammogram warrants a deeper inspection, then a diagnostics mammogram is ordered. Again, your doctor will know what you need.

My journey began with a finding performing routine breast exams on myself. Looking in the mirror at different angles for changes had been part of my care as early as in my twenties. I don't have a family history so when I discovered a concern a few months after my annual screening mammogram, I immediately called by doctor for an appointment and dint wait until the next year. I had no clue at that time that 1 in every 8 women would be diagnosed with breast cancer in their lifetime. My doctor then with my screening mammogram, ordered a diagnostic mammogram and eventually an MRI. This is how to differentiate between a screening mammogram and a diagnostic mammogram. Once an abnormality is seen on a screening mammogram, a diagnostic mammogram is ordered or should be ordered. This is why I advocate and encourage others to get checked by a qualified medical professional. The good news is *breast cancer is 90% curable* if detected early. That's why its important to get regular mammograms. I use my birth month so that way I remember,

During my treatment for breast cancer, I met women in their 20's and 30's. One woman was a 28-year-old wife and mother of 3. There are 64 people in my Tribe and there is no, known history of breast cancer in my family. The only risk factor that seem to fit into my clinical history is that I am a woman. I was over 40 and had ever given birth to children. I was conscientious of what I put into my body. My favorite shopping experience was always at health food markets long before it was a popular thing to do. Five to 6 times a week you could find me in the gym on the elliptical machine, treadmill, or in a aerobics class. My weekend fun would often include a walk 3-4 mile walk in a park and a night of dancing for hours. Needless to say, my dress size was in the single digits. I was not a smoker nor was alcohol part of my routine lifestyle. So naturally when I was diagnosed with breast cancer, I had to take out my rose-colored glasses and start to read and search for answers until the hue of my rose colored glasses became pink.

I have shared in previous chapters how I discovered a change in my breast and immediately called my Doctor. As an advocate and activist my message is get an annual mammogram. Additionally, take action as soon as you can if and when intuition speaks and conveys something needs attention. There is a reason we have something that has been termed 'women's intuition' which is actually the spirit of the living God inside of you.

One of the first questions I had once I was diagnosed and started my treatment plan, was at what point would I become a survivor? I found my answer when I signed up to attend a Brunch hosted by an organization in Philadelphia. The group was called Women of Faith and Hope and was started by Novella Lyons, a breast cancer survivor. Breast cancer statistics indicate that just as many African-American women are diagnosed with breast cancer as Caucasian women, however the death rate is much higher. This arrested my attention and I wanted to know more. I needed to be enlightened and empowered about issues related to breast cancer to reduce the mortality rate.

I saw women, all shades of pecan tan, chestnut beige, toasted almond...with hair, some natural, some synthetic; locked, curled, straight, waved...beautiful! We were present in one space, both the young and the maturely aged. In the quietness of my soul I thought, we truly are "fearfully and wonderfully made'. We are so uniquely fashioned while having a beautiful common thread that connects our very beings. I had not witnessed so many beautiful shades of black, brown, auburn, blond and gray heads styled so attractively. Some of the women looked like my mother, others liked my sisters, some looked like my Aunts, my grandmother, my teachers, my professors, my doctors, my colleagues, my friends and many acquaintances. In so many respects I drew comfort because these women looked like me. The small still voice came, as only it does when I am quite on the inside, "You are never alone". I exhaled, checked my makeup, thanked God for bringing me to this day, clutched my pursed, grabbed my tote bag and moved among the masses to the registration table.

I was diagnosed with breast cancer in May 2004. At this particular event, it was October and I had more rounds of surgery ahead. I had navigated successfully through several appointments with surgeons, oncologist and radiologist. I had traveled to 3 different states and consulted more than 11 different doctors. At my last count, I had logged more than 54 hours of time in a doctor's office, imaging centers or laboratories having x-rays, giving blood to be worked up or in discussions regarding results. I have a leather-bound binder with tabs holding copies of every test, every operating room report, every pathology report, every radiologist report, every journal articles, every bit of nutritional information and all my exercise plans. My life had changed, and I needed to adjust to the changes. This is how my rose-colored glasses turned pink.

What I am endeavoring to share is what I have learned. My prayer and believing is that this information will add to your resources or toolbox for complete and a total recovery if ever diagnosed with breast cancer. Better still, please obtain multiple copies and have them ready to share as a resource with family and friends who may need the encouragement that they too can live well beyond breast cancer. Why? Because it is the absolute will of God that we each be healed and made whole. I found doctors that I could relate to, who were trustworthy and who I could trust to enter into a partnership with me. That is why I obtained a second and even a third opinion.

My advocacy messaging advises maintaining journals and speaking to other women in the fight to recover their health. I kept a diary and recorded my thoughts. When I couldn't think of anything to write or perhaps wasn't inspired, I looked to others and captured the stories of other women affected by this disease because I just wanted to know as much as I could. Some of these women were quite young and others quite old. From the younger women, I learned the importance of knowing family history and to keep speaking and searching for doctors who will listen. One friend is alive today because her doctor didn't dismiss her request for a mammogram although she was only 32 years old. I have learned from organizations such as, Women of Faith and Hope in Philadelphia or the Brem Foundation in the Washington, DC area. There are many others as well. Check your local area for education and support. Know that if there is a first-degree history of breast cancer in your family, meaning your grandmother, mother, or sister, have been diagnosed with breast cancer, then talk to a doctor who will listen, about starting your breast cancer screening earlier than age 40. If your doctor is unable to hear you, find one who will. Don't let the circumstances or situation talk you out of thinking pink! Don't stop until you find rose colored glasses that are tinted pink.

Advocate for a mammogram that uses the latest technology called 3D or Tomo. Tomo is short for DBT or dense breast tomosynthesis. If you live in an area where 3D is not available, know that a 2D mammogram is the gold standard at the time of this writing. In the United States, governing bodies have ruled 2D as the gold standard. A gold standard is the standard of care that every woman should have annually, although, it is agreed, 3D is superior. Talk to you doctor and ask them for more information.

Breast density and the makeup of the tissue that Radiologist examine is so important it bears a mention here. Know you personal risk factors for breast cancer and also know your breast density. Breast density can only be determined by a mammogram. It has nothing to do with the size or the feel of your breast. Talk to your doctor or consult a Radiologist about your breast density.

One woman, Nancy Capella, MD changed the way women are imaged when it comes to mammography based on her own experience. As a doctor, she routinely scheduled her annual mammograms, only to find out, just months after a mammogram, she was diagnosed with stage 4 breast cancer! She wondered how could this be? She was told because her breasts were dense it was difficult to visualize. Single-highhandedly, she set out to set the world on fire to make sure everyone knew the importance of breast density and how supplemental screen may save your life!

One person can change the world. One person can make a difference. Jesus Christ, Nancy Capella and me too. I too want my life to count and help as many people as I can. Women with dense breasts, but no other risk factors for breast cancer, are considered to have a higher risk of breast cancer than average. If they don't seem informed, don't be surprised. Find another doctor! Early detection saves lives and despite concerns about detecting cancer in dense breasts, mammograms are an effective screening tool.

8

Write it Down, Review it Often and Make it Happen

I feel naked if I don't have a pen and piece of paper with me or near by as I living my life out loud. I've often wanted to be able to capture ideas and thoughts that would help me cast and model my life. I had long since noted that inspiration and ideas come at the most unusual and unlikely times, so I have maintained a habit of jotting it down over the years. I have a collection of hard bound books that have recorded my thoughts that go back to several decades. In this age of instant and immediate gratification, there are a few like myself that enjoy words in print.

Writing down your thoughts is incredibly important. It allows for a review. Capturing thoughts in written form in some way for retrieval serves as fuel to make things happen. I liken this process or habit to that of laying cement. After watching my husband prepare to lay cement, it was similar to making a cake, He mixed solid material with wet material and the end result was a final product that was sustainable. But unlike baking a cake, there seemed to be a time element to get the cement in place before it started to set. During this time my husband told me that once the cement sets or hardens it can later bear weight or could be walked on. In between the preparation stages and the set up was a moment in time when

I put my hand in the cement when my husband wasn't looking. A few minutes later when I looked at the square he had just finished, my handprint was gone! The impression had been loss in minutes. I learned to capture my thoughts with paper and pen so as happens often enough, the thoughts disappear and if not written down, may be lost forever. Writing things down allows for your thoughts to be set and later reviewed in a semi-permanent form.

The number 8 has been attributed a significant number denoting a new beginning. The number 40 can be understood as 5 cycles of 8. Five has been associated with God's grace. When I turned 40, I started writing more and writing detailed thoughts. My hands often tired long before the inspiration would cease so I invested in a computer. A Gateway computer and that was indeed exactly what it became, a gateway to start writing down what God was doing in my life. The company doesn't exist, but I kept the Gateway keyboard as a reminder of how this book began. I even still have a stack of the floppy disc that it began on. Those discs have been transcribed and helped capture the backbone of this book. The abundant grace of God that has preserved my life is unspeakable but what I can tell you is, God is an ever-present help in your time of need.

I've gone back to my journals many times. At times to recall a specific situation and at other times to review accomplishments. A total sum of my life experience directed my steps in such a way I was experiencing a new beginning. A pattern of applied life lessons emerged. A re-occurring them was present and that of thankfulness.

Being thankful and continuously cultivating an attitude of gratitude has gotten me to this point. No matter what my situation was, I could draw breath life and that was proof enough that God would see me through whatever the challenge may be. Some of the things I was thankful for were things like the opportunity to get it right and thankful that I was able to recognize when I had wronged someone and was able to apologize. I was and am thankful I have been successful and that God has made His grace available to cover my life such that the harsh impact of consequences did not come crashing down on my head. I had to sign a release form each time I had surgery stating that If I died, it would not be the hospitals fault. Chemotherapy is inter-cellular poison to stop cells from dividing. I was and am thankful the therapy didn't kill me. I'm just thankful to live and have the benefit of people who have offered love and support, whether it be family, friends or total strangers. Chronically my journey through a diagnosis of breast cancer in written form and going back to review it brought me to the con-clusion that my story needed to be told written down.

I was diagnosed with breast cancer in my 40's. During my last round of chemotherapy, I wrote down a few goals to achieve before the year ended. Two are worth mentioning. The first was to burn a CD of what I'll call songs that helped me endure and maintain my happy as I was going through the fight of my life. The second goal I wrote down was to move into a new house. Once chemo and radiation were finished, I wanted to start a new life in a new place as I knew my life would never be the same. I wrote these things down and reviewed what I had written quite often. Now it was time to make it happen.

Going through breast cancer treatment or any challenge requires that you keep and maintain a positive attitude. I cannot emphasis this enough. I actually purchase a book with 100 jokes and mem-orized so many as I wanted to share them with my Oncology nurses. I am so grateful for these people who provide care when others are in crisis. They are everyday heroes. It was important that I not only brought them lunches and treats to show my appreciation, but I also wanted to stay light-hear ted during the procedures. I wrote this in my diary and I'm sharing it here because it's a testament of how important it is to write your thoughts down and not just your thoughts, but also your goals. I prefer pen and paper because it last longer that my memory. Even when electronics fail, as experienced with diminished and disruptive server and bandwidth issues was during COVID or with mobile devices when service was nonexistent during 9-11, I always need a way to access my thoughts, ideas and goals

Driving to work and to appointments during my treatments, I would play a CD that I had burned on my computer of what I later titled my survivor playlist. The first song was Destiny's Child I'm a survivor. I would sing to the top of my lungs in the shower and in my car that I was a survivor and I was not going to give up! I would push the replay button at least 3 to 5 times on Yolanda Adams's the battle is not mine but the lords reminding myself that I was not in this alone. I won't go through my entire playlist but will encourage you who are going through a difficult time to make your own playlist and put it in a reproducible form so you don't have to search for it or remember the names of the songs. Writing these things down and making it happen were keys to my surviving breast cancer,

My husband has always been my biggest supporter and no matter what ideas I come up with, he helps me vet them and then stands back as God and I go to work. It was no different when I said we needed to move to a new house. We had been in our home 5 years and had it perfect for us. Nevertheless, he agreed. Within 3 months our home was sold, and we moved to new house. I had written the goal down of a new house and my husband fully agreed that it would do us both good to have a new beginning. After all, we had a new lease on life.

It's important to have a special place to work in your own home. I have had my own home office for more than 2 decades. I have inspirational quotes, awards, Degrees, and a white board hanging on the 4 walls. This has been a vital part of my writing it down, reviewing it often and making it happen. Whether you have a home office or not isn't as important as having a special place to work on your goals. If you don't have your own home office today doesn't mean you will never have one. It's important to have a place to incubate your ideas and projects. Set a goal, Write it down. Review it Often and make it happen.

It never matters how long it takes to accomplish your goals but that you accomplish them. This book has been in my head and heart longer than I would like to think. I have had to power my way through to get it done and I thank all those mentioned in the pages that poured into my life to make it happen. I am eternally thankful that you have stayed with me to the end and gave my story a listen. Every one has a story. You have read mine. What's yours?

THE END

About this Book

Beyond breast cancer is where so many of us are who have been impacted by this disease. This has happened partly because we learn more about ourselves and are not afraid to take the power to make life saving decisions for ourselves. I chose the word 'beyond' with emphasis on describing how to arrive at or get to the further side of a diagnosis. I have had the opportunity to meet amazing Doctors. Many choose the profession looking to do the greatest good but we must always remember they too are imperfect. Doctors are practicing medicine but we are the experts of our bodies and have the most knowledge about ourselves. With this understanding, we can look well beyond the time point of a diagnosis of breast cancer.

One of the greatest keys to looking well beyond breast cancer or any situation that tried to hinder you from walking into your destiny is to remember that we were amazing creations made by God. We are fashioned in His image and each one of us is uniquely special. If you don't already know yourself and your purpose and what you are to be while here on earth, take time to quietly reflect and consider your life. We are so much more than our physical bodies designed to live well beyond breast cancer.

Appendix I: Advocate For Yourself

While knowing your screening options and risk factors is critical, being aware of—and demanding—your breast health rights may be the difference between life and death.

Breast Health Bill Of Rights

- **You have the right** to an annual mammogram after the age of 40—and sometimes earlier, depending on your risk factors.

- **You have the right** to have your mammogram read by doctors who spend the majority of their time reading mammograms.

- **You have the right** to additional screenings (including 3-D mammograms) if you have dense breast tissue.

- **You have the right** to see a physician within two days after a mass is detected.

- **You have the right** to a non-surgical, needle breast biopsy.

- **You have the right** to fast biopsy results, usually within five days.

- **You have the right** to an MRI or breast-specific gamma imaging (BSGI) if you are a newly diagnosed breast cancer patient.

You have the right to advocate for yourself, because you know yourself better than anyone else.

Appendix II

Here are my favorite doctors, as I have a personal connection with them. There are many others and I am happy to help you locate resources near you if you need a referral:

- Dr. Kevin Fox – Director, Rena Rowan Breast Center or Dr. Susan Domchek, Director, MacDonald Women's Cancer Risk Evaluation Center | University of Penn, **Philadelphia, PA**

- Dr. Rachel Brem – Director, George Washington University Breast Center in **Washington, DC.**

- Dr. Susan Harvey- Director, John Hopkins Breast Center **Baltimore, MD**

- Dr. Kathy Schilling, Director, Lynn Women's Health & Wellness Institute, **Boca Raton FL**- great way to vacation and get a complete check up by some amazing women! They have yoga, dietitians, general practitioners and more! If ever in Florida, make this stop to get red carpet service!

- Dr. Jennifer Harvey- Director, University of VA Breast Center **Charlottesville, VA**

- Dr. Elise Berman Inova | Fairfax Radiology **Fairfax, VA**

- Dr. Connie Lehman, Director, Breast Center, Massachusetts General Hospital, **Boston, MA**

- Dr. Georgia Spear| NorthShore University Health Breast Imaging, **Chicago IL**
- Dr. Angelica Robinson | Director of Breast Imaging | UTMB **Galveston, TX**

Use this information to receive the best available. I am building this into my website so please visit often. Feedback is always appreciated as to how to share this messaging. My website is just getting started so it is not fully baked, however, visit me here:

www.breastcancersurvivorship.com

CARMEN MARSHALL | CHIEF VISIONARY | BREAST CANCER SURVIVORSHIP